They Came to Wisconsin

Julia Pferdehirt

Wisconsin Historical Society Press
Madison, Wisconsin

Published by the Wisconsin Historical Society Press

Photographs identified with PH, WHi, or WHS are from the Society's collections; address inquiries about such photos to the Curator, Visual Materials Archive, at the above address.

Publications of the Wisconsin Historical Society Press are available at quantity discounts for promotions, fund raising, and educational use. Write to the above address for more information.

Printed in the United States of America

Book design and badger illustrations by Jill Bremigan

Front cover photo of the *George Washington* from the Richard Faber Collection. Back cover photo of Zer Yang and Xay Her from the *Milwaukee Journal* (4/17/87); WHS CF 329166.

**Other Titles in the
New Badger History Series**
(Includes classroom texts and teacher guides)

*Digging and Discovery:
Wisconsin Archaeology*

*Learning from the Land:
Wisconsin Land Use*

*Working with Water:
Wisconsin Waterways*

Native People of Wisconsin
(coming in 2003)

07 06 05 04 03   5 4 3 2 1

Library of Congress Cataloging-in-Publication Data

Pferdehirt, Julia.
    They came to Wisconsin / by Julia Pferdehirt and Bobbie Malone.
        p.   cm. — (The new badger history series)
    ISBN 0-87020-328-2
    1. Immigrants—Wisconsin—History—Juvenile literature. 2. Wisconsin—Emigration and immigration—History—Juvenile literature. [1. Immigrants—History. 2. Wisconsin—Emigration and immigration—History.]
I. Pferdehirt, Julia, 1952– II. Title. III. Series.

F590.A1 P48 2002
977.5—dc21

                                                                                    2001018398

Contents

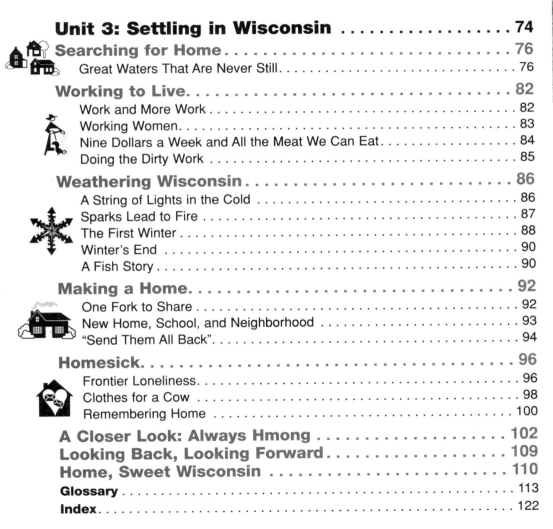

World Origins

People moved to Wisconsin from all over the world. In this book you'll meet people who came from the places you see highlighted on this map.

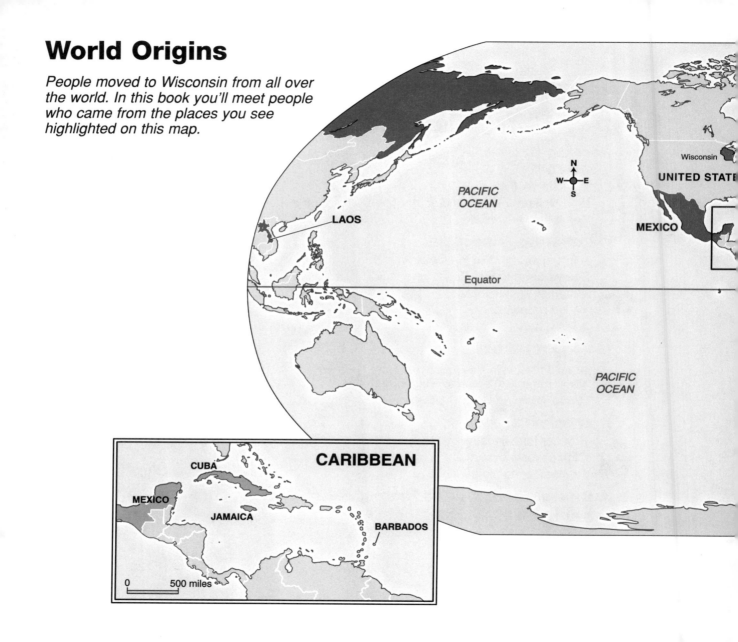

PACIFIC OCEAN

Wisconsin

UNITED STATE

LAOS

MEXICO

Equator

PACIFIC OCEAN

CARIBBEAN

CUBA

MEXICO

JAMAICA

BARBADOS

0   500 miles

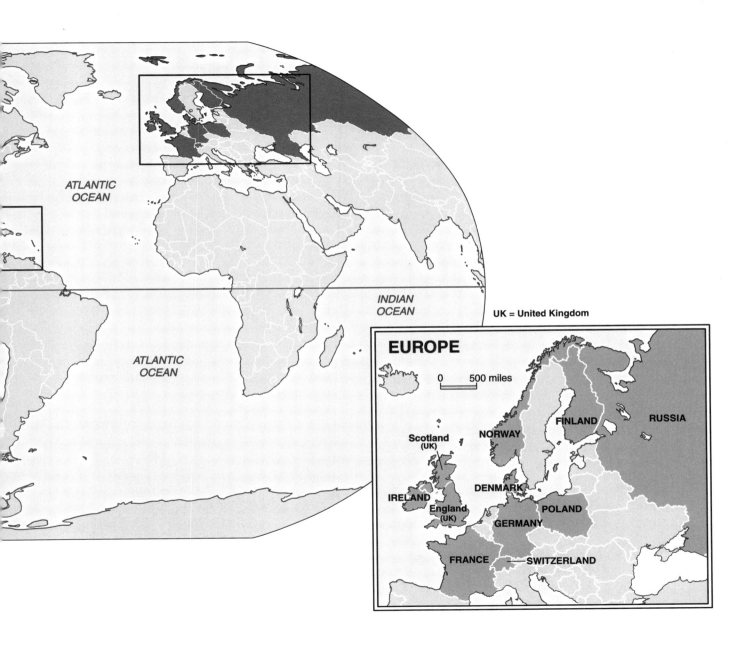

ATLANTIC
OCEAN

ATLANTIC
OCEAN

INDIAN
OCEAN

UK = United Kingdom

EUROPE

0   500 miles

NORWAY

FINLAND

RUSSIA

Scotland
(UK)

IRELAND

DENMARK

England
(UK)

POLAND

GERMANY

FRANCE   SWITZERLAND

A delivery wagon in Madison in the early 1900s

WHS Archives, CF 6437

Introduction: A Book of Real Stories

A moving van is parked in a driveway, half-filled with cardboard boxes and furniture. There are lots of boxes stacked around the house, too. Everyone is very busy packing, carrying boxes, or loading them into the van. It's moving day!

There are many reasons to move, and almost every family moves at some time. Moving and settling in a new place can be exciting, but it can also be a little scary. Sometimes it's hard to be the new person on the block or at school. You may never have wanted to move, but maybe your mom's job transferred her to a new city, or your dad wanted you all to live closer to the rest of his family.

Every day people move from community to community or even from country to country. During most of the 1800s and throughout the 1900s, millions of people were on the move. Like streams flowing into a great river, people came from all over the world to America. Each group brought its own stories, its own language, and its own culture. Together, they shaped our country into what it is today—a nation made more interesting because of the many people living here. Some of these people headed for Wisconsin, and their stories and cultures are now part of our state history.

Long, long before the 1800s, different groups of Indian people lived all over the land we now call Wisconsin. These groups, such as the Menominee,

WHS Archives, CF 6437

Compare this photo from the 1950s with the one above. What differences in how people move can you find fifty years later?

2

Ho-Chunk, Potawatomi, and Ojibwe tribes, are important to Wisconsin history, and their stories can be found in other books. *They Came to Wisconsin* is about the people who arrived here later. It is about Indian tribes like the Mohican, who came here *after* 1800. It is also about many non-Indian people from all over the Americas, Europe, and Asia, who arrived after 1800.

These "newcomers" decided to leave their homes, made long trips to reach Wisconsin, and then settled here. Each unit of this book contains *real* stories that tell why people left their homes, how they traveled, and what they found when they arrived. No matter why people left or how they got here, they came to Wisconsin in search of a better life for their families, especially for their children.

How Historians Work

They Came to Wisconsin contains many stories. History writers search for the real stories that tell what the past was like. How do historians find these stories? First they read books written about the past. Then historians look at **historical resources** (firsthand information) created during the time period they are studying. These historical resources help historians piece together a picture of the past. Sometimes historians find paper **documents** (**doc** u ments, printed or handwritten letters, journals, diaries, drawings, or photographs) that people made in the past. Sometimes historians learn about people's lives through **artifacts** (**ar** tih facts, objects like clothing, tools, or toys) that people used in the past.

Historians search for stories. But not all stories are written down. Some stories are told and retold whenever people come together, especially at weddings, funerals, family reunions, and holidays. Historians might interview family members who have heard and remember stories that have been passed down. Historians also talk to

George Stoner's 1862 diary. In 1837, at the age of seven, Stoner moved to Madison. He was one of the city's earliest residents.

WHS Archives, CF 3612

Sometimes people learn history from listening to older people's stories, like the children in this photo, taken in Sturgeon Bay around 1905.

people about their experiences. All these historical resources add to the picture of what happened in the past.

But how do you know when you are reading something that someone in the past really wrote or said?

Real Words from the Past

When you read **fiction** (a made-up story) you often see words with quotation marks around them. The quotation marks let you know that someone is saying those words out loud. But when you read a **history book** (a story that really happened), quotation marks have another meaning.

In this book, quotation marks around words mean that a real person *actually* said or wrote down these words. Quotation marks tell you that what you're reading is a piece of that person's story. They give you a sense of what that person was like and what he or she thought and said.

If we tried to use every word from people's stories, this book would be too long. When words are left out you will see an ellipsis, which looks like this . . .

Sometimes the words that people used in the past are unfamiliar or hard to understand. To help make the writing clear, you will see brackets [ ] around words that help explain or define the meaning of another word.

Read this next paragraph and see the quotation marks, ellipses, and brackets:

> Rubie said, "My first impression of Beloit? Well, it was 1,000 miles north and I was just ten. My grandfather went to find a place to live. Then, snow! Snow! It was so cold. And I went to school. Not a Mississippi school, but a good school with art and music . . . **[In Mississippi we had]** eight grades in two rooms . . . with a leaky roof. And the white children went to school in a brick building."

They Came to Wisconsin contains stories from many people who came from many places. Before airplanes, people who wanted to come to Wisconsin had to arrive at the U.S. border first, because Wisconsin is in the middle of the North American continent. All the people in this book finally settled in Wisconsin. Not all of them kept complete stories of their experiences. Sometimes letters and journals tell only part of a story.

In this book, you'll meet some of these people once and others many times. At the end of each unit, you'll find one complete story of leaving, traveling, and settling. Now you can settle in and enjoy the book!

The Boat came to at Sheboygan for wood. I did not go on shore but from the Boat the place had a pleasant aspect the site of the village being situated on the Buildings & stir about the Wharf gave indication

WHS Archives

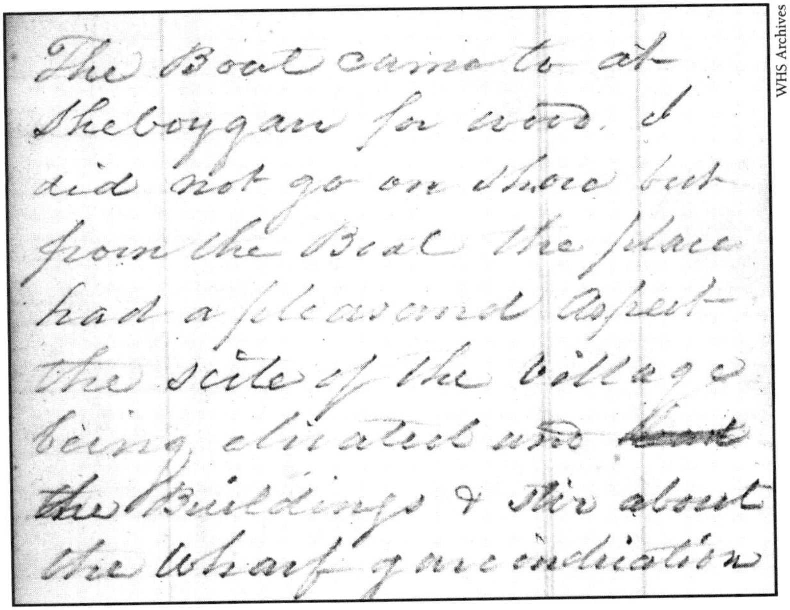

Bela B. Hyde wrote about her trip from western New York across the Great Lakes to Wisconsin in the summer of 1848. Can you read her handwriting where she writes about the stop in Sheboygan?

Unit 1
Deciding to Leave

♦ ♦ ♦

What is your dream? Love? Adventure? Money? In the 1800s and the early 1900s, many people followed their dreams to Wisconsin. Just like today, making the decision to leave one home for another meant thinking hard. Would life in a new home be better than life in the old? Imagining a better life is the kind of dreaming that leads to decisions.

People came to our state from every corner of the world and for all kinds of reasons. The three main reasons people came to Wisconsin were to find opportunity, to leave behind hardship and hunger, and to escape injustice. In this unit you will meet people who came for each of these reasons, and some who came for a combination of reasons.

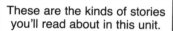

These are the kinds of stories you'll read about in this unit.

 Opportunities for a Better Life

 Leaving Hunger and Hardship Behind

 Escaping Injustice and Cruelty

TIMELINE

These are the people you will meet in this unit, and these are the dates when they were making their decisions to come to Wisconsin.

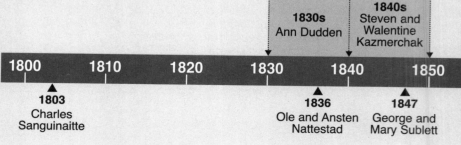

1830s Ann Dudden

1840s Steven and Walentine Kazmerchak

1800   1810   1820   1830   1840   1850

1803 Charles Sanguinaitte

1836 Ole and Ansten Nattestad

1847 George and Mary Sublett

6

WHS Archives, WHi(X3)13380

Immigrants came to Wisconsin to make a better life for themselves.

1891
Kanter Family

| 1860 | 1870 | 1880 | 1890 | 1900 | 1910 | 1920 |

1860
Svein
Nilsson

1890s
Clara Brown

1917
Rubie Bond

Opportunities for a Better Life

Once people heard stories of living well in America, they began to look at their own lives. They began to realize how difficult their lives were. Dreaming of America meant dreaming of making a change. Dreaming of leaving for America meant the chance to look for something better.

Wisconsin

France

Map by Amelia Janes/Mike Gallagher, Midwest Educational Graphics

A Dream of Riches

Nearly four hundred years ago, **voyageurs** (voy a **jurs,** French Canadian boatmen) followed their dreams to Wisconsin. These French Canadians were explorers, fur trappers, traders, and lovers of all things wild and adventurous. Some came from wealthy, educated families. Others were farm boys who wanted more in their lives than plowing fields and milking cows.

WHS Archives, CF 5587

Voyageurs were some of the first European travelers in North America. Since they were here before roads, they had to use canoes to get around. Native people taught the voyageurs how to build birchbark canoes. These lightweight canoes could carry bundles of trade goods and furs over dangerous rapids.

Voyageurs came to America for fur. In Europe, beaver and mink were popular for fancy gentlemen's hats and ladies' collars. In America, beavers and mink lived in the wild. So the voyageurs came to trap animals, sell furs, and get rich.

In 1803, one voyageur, Charles Sanguinaitte (**san** gween et), hauled the

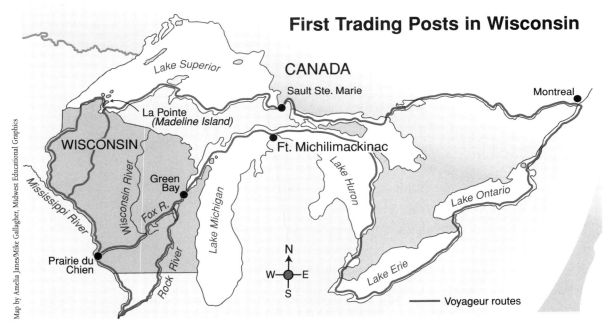

First Trading Posts in Wisconsin

From the late 1600s through the early 1800s, voyageurs made journeys through Wisconsin, following routes shown on this map. The first trading posts here were at Green Bay and Prairie du Chien.

skins of 510 beavers, 437 wildcats, 245 bears, 133 deer, 97 bear cubs, 30 muskrats, 26 otters, 11 lynx, and 1 mink to a trading post in Prairie du Chien. His pay was 1,173 silver **shillings** (English money)—a small fortune! Charles was a wealthy man, at least until he spent his new fortune on rum, card games, and new clothes.

The voyageurs dreamed of wealth and adventure. Other people dreamed of things that mattered most to them, like owning their own land, working for themselves, or working for better pay.

Ansten Nattestad

What Kind of Life Is This?

Two Norwegian brothers, Ole and Ansten Nattestad (**oh** lee and **on** sten **nah** tih stahd), worked on a rocky little farm in Norway, trying to scratch out a living. They worked summer and winter, sunrise to sunset, milking, hauling, plowing, and planting. Maybe this year the harvest would be good, they hoped. Maybe this year.

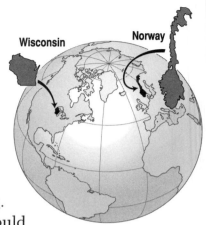

Wisconsin   Norway

People in Norway were forced to farm on rocky, hilly land. In Wisconsin in the mid- to late 1800s, it was easy to get good land.

Every spring they borrowed money from the landowner to plant seed. They later had to pay back even more than they borrowed. The Nattestads plowed and planted. They counted the newborn goats and prayed for a calf or two. Still, at the end of every year, they had less money and owed the landowner more. They must have wondered, *what kind of life is this?*

Then, in the fall of 1836, the brothers crossed the mountains on a sheep-buying trip to the seaside city of Stavanger (stuh **vahng** ur). "We heard much talk about a country which was called America," Ansten wrote. "This was the first time we heard this word. We saw letters written by Norwegians . . . they had gone in spite of threats and warnings about slavery, death, and disease."

Ole and Ansten returned home. All winter they talked and wondered. Could it possibly be true that America had no landowner to say where you could work and how you could earn a living? Could they believe the stories of cheap land and fair laws? That winter, they caught something called "America Fever."

In 1839, Ole Nattestad wrote about the journey that he and his brother made to reach the United States. As you can tell from the cover of his book, he wrote it in Norwegian. How do we know the Nattestads' story? Someone had to translate the book into English.

11

Lägsta Priset från
Malmö, Göteborg och Stockholm till New York
$27.

Med **Bremer-Linien** sändes passagerare på de snabbaste ångare två gänger hvarje vecka från Bremen och anländer i

CHICAGO på 11 till 13 Dagar,

och till alla andra platser på den kortast möjlaga tid.

På **Bremer-Liniens** ångare blifva passagerare försedde med de bästa lifsmedel och beqwämligheter. Behandlingen ombord är i alla delar utmärkt.

En Million Passagerare

äro under de sista 25 åren befordrade öfver Atlanterhafvet med Bremer-Linien.

Man vända sig till

OELRICHS & CO.,
General Agenter,
2 BOWLING GREEN, NEW YORK.
ELLER TILL

CHARLES BURMEISTER, Agent,
FRANKFURT, Mich.

This flyer, written in Swedish, advertises a trip from Stockholm, Sweden, to New York in the 1800s. How much does the ticket cost? What other words can you read?

America Fever

When you think of having a fever, you probably think of being sick and missing school. Fever can also mean excitement. During the 1800s, people all over Europe heard stories about America. They began to think about **emigrating** (**em** mi gra ting, leaving one country to move to another). America seemed like a magical place—a promised land. People began to dream and plan. Their friends said they had caught America fever. People spoke of America like it was heaven. For example, some called America a land of milk and honey, a place with plenty of food and great promise.

America fever! In about 1860, American fever hit Snasa (**snah** suh), Norway. Svein (svine) Nilsson wrote, "Half of the people in Snasa had lost their senses. Nothing was talked of except the land that flows with milk and honey. Our **pastor** [church leader] . . . tried to cure the fever." Pastor Rynning begged the people not to leave Norway. His **sermons** (talks) were filled with stories of dangerous ocean crossings, sharks, shipwrecks, sickness, and thieves on the docks in New York City. Pastor Rynning warned people to stay home. He said America was a terrible place where wild animals prowled the forests and blizzards howled all winter. The warnings did no good. America fever had struck, and every day it increased.

America fever spread from country to country. First people heard stories or read letters describing America as a paradise. Then people began to dream of America. They sold their possessions and used their savings to buy tickets for the ocean crossing. By the time the fever cooled, more than one hundred years had passed, and people from every corner of the globe had arrived on American soil. Many thousands of those people came to Wisconsin.

In many places around the world today, people are still likely to catch America fever. Some of them may one day come to Wisconsin.

Leaving Hunger and Hardship Behind

Many people came to Wisconsin because of **poverty** (**pahv** ur tee, being very poor). This hardship meant more than just wearing last year's clothes or having bills to pay. It meant dressing in rags, carving wooden shoes, or going barefoot. It meant cold nights without a stick of wood to feed the fire. It meant that a starving young girl might need to sew a hem in her **petticoat** (slip or underskirt) so she could hide grain she stole from the landlord. Often, it meant hunger.

These wooden shoes were made in Horicon about 1880–1890.

Photo by Joel Heiman

Many people didn't want to leave the homelands they loved, but hunger and poverty forced them out. "The heart pleaded no, but the stomach commanded yes," wrote one newcomer fresh from Finland.

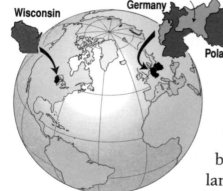

Map by Amelia Janes/Mike Gallagher, Midwest Educational Graphics

Working Like Animals

The Kazmerchak (**kaz** mur chak) family lived on only $20 a year in **Prussia** (**prush** ah, once a country, now a part of Germany and Poland). Like the Nattestads in Norway, two of the Kazmerchak brothers, Steven and Walentine, worked for a wealthy landowner. He owned everything in sight: the houses, barns, fields, and even the deer in the forest. The landowner might as well have owned the people, too. They lived like slaves.

Each year the landowner gave the Kazmerchaks "a bushel of wheat, a bushel of peas, maybe twelve bushels of rye, and the use of a garden plot about an acre and a half in size." That food, the garden plot, and $20 were supposed to feed and clothe the whole family for a year.

The Kazmerchak brothers worked the landowner's fields, harvesting wheat to fill his already full barns. At home, they ate potatoes, cabbage, peas, and tough, black bread. All the fine, white flour was sent to the landowner's kitchen to be baked into soft, white bread for his family.

When the long hours in the landowner's fields were finally over, Steven and Walentine Kazmerchak could farm their own small garden. It was tending this garden that made Steven and Walentine finally ask themselves, *what kind of life is this?*

It was spring. To level their garden, the Kazmerchak brothers borrowed a heavy **drag** (a tool pulled across the ground to smooth it) from the landowner. His stables were filled with horses, but the brothers didn't dare ask to use one. Since they had no horses to pull the drag, the brothers chained themselves to it. Then, slowly and painfully, they pulled the heavy drag across the field.

Drawing by Middleton High School student Scott Poniewaz

Even the brothers' strong backs weren't made to pull such weight. They had to stop often just to breathe. Every muscle hurt. Still, the job had to be done if the garden was to be planted. Next winter, they would need to eat the vegetables they were planting. So they pulled and rested, pulled and rested.

Pulling the log drag was no job for a human!

At the end of a long pull, Steven and Walentine stopped to straighten their aching backs. There, leaning on the stone fence, was the landowner himself, just watching them. Watching! Fifty years later in Kewaunee, Steven Kazmerchak still remembered the landowner's face and his own angry feelings. He wrote, "That fellow just stood there and watched us . . . watched us . . . like a couple of animals! . . . That was what started us for America."

The Great Hunger

London Illustrated News, 1849

In Ireland, as in Norway, Prussia, and many other countries around the world, a few people owned every inch of farmland. Everyone else worked for those few wealthy men. The rich got richer and the poor stayed poor. People went hungry. What could be worse than barely surviving while the landowners got rich?

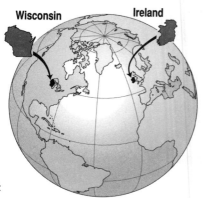

Wisconsin   Ireland

Map by Amelia Janes/Mike Gallagher,
Midwest Educational Graphics

This drawing shows Bridget O'Donnell and her children during the Great Hunger. This starving Irish family had to beg for food.

There was something worse. In 1830 **cholera** (**cah** lur ah, a quick-spreading disease that killed many) struck. Then the following year, 1831, Ireland's potato crop failed! A disease called blight made the potatoes rot in the fields. Without potatoes, people weren't just hungry, they *starved*. They died by the thousands and, also by the thousands, they fled to America.

16

This Irish peasant cottage had a "beehive" roof. In what ways is this cottage different from the one on the Norwegian farm on page 10?

WHS Archives, CF 403

Ann Dudden was one of those starving Irish children. As an old woman, more than seventy years later in Oconto, she still remembered what happened to her family. "They were poor. They were **wretchedly** (**retch** ed lee, very unhappily) poor. . . . My grandfather's people were put off of the **estate** (landlord's property). They didn't own a foot of ground." Where could they go? There were jobs in the cities, but Ann Dudden's grandfather was a country sheepherder. What job could a sheepherder find in a city?

Ann Dudden's grandfather and uncle died of starvation and illness. Her mother and sisters couldn't even earn enough to feed themselves. In **desperation** (des per **a** shun, hopelessness), the Dudden family sold everything and went to America.

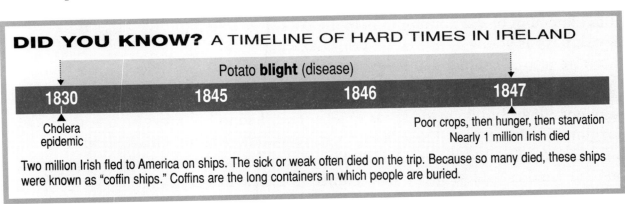

DID YOU KNOW? A TIMELINE OF HARD TIMES IN IRELAND

Potato **blight** (disease)

| 1830 | 1845 | 1846 | 1847 |

Cholera epidemic

Poor crops, then hunger, then starvation
Nearly 1 million Irish died

Two million Irish fled to America on ships. The sick or weak often died on the trip. Because so many died, these ships were known as "coffin ships." Coffins are the long containers in which people are buried.

Escaping Injustice and Cruelty

At different times and places all over the world, people have been **persecuted** (**pur** seh kyoo ted). That means they were treated cruelly and unfairly because of their religion, skin color, or ideas. They had to leave their homes in order to survive.

Ashes, Feathers, and Broken Glass

Across Russia after 1881, the government of the **tsar** (zar, king) allowed organized cruelty and violence against Jews called **pogroms** (po **groms**). Everyone who was Jewish was in danger. Wild mobs attacked and killed Jewish people. These mobs often burned **synagogues** (**sin** uh gogz, places where Jews worship) and Jewish neighborhoods. Soldiers and police either joined in or did nothing to help the Jews. Jewish boys as young as five or six years old were taken from their families and forced to join the army.

Map by Amelia Janes/Mike Gallagher,
Midwest Educational Graphics

Russia's laws took away Jews' rights and freedom. Jews could not own land. They were not allowed to do many kinds of jobs. They had to live apart from non-Jews in a region called The Pale. These laws got more and more strict. Finally, Jewish butchers like Azriel Kanter were forbidden to work at all. How would they put food on their families' tables? Many Jews wanted to escape to a better life.

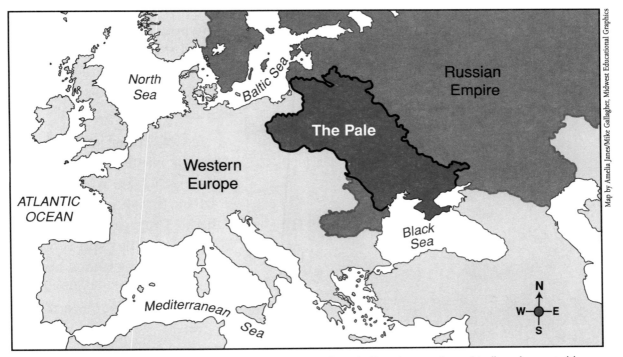

This map shows the Pale of Settlement, where most Jews in Russia were forced to live. Jews could not own land, and many jobs were closed to them. America promised many kinds of freedom.

Azriel and Rosa Kanter's young daughter, Cele, couldn't understand what was happening. Little Cele asked, "Mama, why would they [the Russian mobs] want to drive us out?" Her mother answered, "Because we are Jews." "But we are good, honest Jews!" Cele said. The Russian mobs didn't seem to notice or care.

In their hearts, people asked themselves little Cele's sad question, "Why would they want to drive us out?" The answer? Just because they were Jews. Many Russians

19

Illustration by Susan Manske

Pogroms destroyed people's property—and sometimes destroyed their lives.

were poor and angry. They turned their anger and hatred against the Jews, whose culture and religion they did not understand.

Azriel Kanter kept a diary. Once he wrote about the village of Corfu, where thirteen Jewish men were killed. "Their property was reduced to ashes and rubble. They were surrounded and imprisoned in their own homes, then driven out to the last one."

Azriel and his family could not go on living in Russia. His friends said he should leave for America. He agreed.

Clara Brown's family also lived through the pogroms in Russia. She never forgot the night one of these mobs came to her village in the late 1800s. "We ran into the woods," she remembered. Clara's family stayed hidden for days. When they finally crept out of the woods, it looked like a war had been fought in their village. Doors were smashed. Smoke still rose from burned buildings. Broken glass was everywhere.

"It looked like winter, from the feathers of the Jewish feather beds," Clara remembered. "And glass. . . . Every window in the houses was broken."

Some people hadn't been lucky enough to hide in the woods. Clara remembered men shouting, babies crying, and injured people everywhere. Everyone was so afraid. "I was only eleven years old, going on twelve. I didn't know what it was all about. I heard everybody was crying. Everybody was **mourning** [**morn** ing, feeling deeply sad]. There was not a smile for many months." Like the Kanters, Clara Brown's family left everything behind and escaped to America.

Heading North

Some people had to escape injustice right here in the United States. Rubie Bond was only ten years old in 1917 when she and her family left for Wisconsin. They were not emigrating from another country. They were **migrating** (**my** grating, moving from community to community in the same country). They came from Pontotoc (**pon** tuh tok), Mississippi. Like the Nattestads in Norway and the Kazmerchaks in Prussia, Rubie's papa and grandfather did not own the farms where they worked. Rubie's papa and grandfather were **sharecroppers.** Sharecroppers were

Map by Amelia Janes/Mike Gallagher, Midwest Educational Graphics

so poor that they had no money to rent the land they farmed. To pay the landowner for rent and seed, sharecroppers first had to harvest a crop. After they sold the crop, they paid the landowner a share of the money they made. The landowner took his share, whether the crop was big or small. Just like the Nattestad and Kazmerchak brothers, each year Rubie's papa had less, and the landowner had more.

Cotton was one of the most common crops grown by sharecroppers in the South. Sharecroppers didn't have a lot of money. All family members—even the young children—had to work in the fields.

A sharecropper's whole family had to work. Rubie's family worked for Mr. Stegall, a cruel man. Rubie never forgot how Mr. Stegall treated her blind Grandma Carolyn. "Being blind, she was, of course, of no use . . . for working." Mr. Stegall refused to let Grandma Carolyn remain on his property. Sixty years later Rubie remembered how it "broke my mother's heart. I was my grandmother's favorite grandchild and I never saw her again."

When Rubie's papa found work on another farm, Mr. Stegall let the Bonds carry away only the clothes they were wearing. But Rubie's papa had dreams. He didn't intend to be a sharecropper forever.

Then one day Rubie's papa heard about jobs in Wisconsin. A man from Beloit arrived in Pontotoc, looking for African American men who were willing to work hard. He did not let the landowners know that he was promising sharecroppers good jobs in Beloit. The landowner would have been angry, because he did not want to lose the people who were working his land. But Rubie's mama and papa wanted a better life for themselves and their family. They packed their bags, sold the few things they owned, and left.

Sharecroppers like the Bonds were not the first African Americans to migrate north to Wisconsin. In the years before 1865, some African Americans escaped from slavery in the South to free states like Wisconsin. In the next section, "A Closer Look," you'll get to know one such family, the Subletts. Injustice *pushed* them from the South. A chance to live as free people *pulled* them to Wisconsin.

WHS Archives, PL 4624

Tom Wright and his family were sharecroppers in southeast Missouri around 1938. What details in the photograph tell you how poor they were?

A Closer Look

As a Slave, Your Life Is Not Your Own

In the years before 1865, some white people in the United States owned African American slaves. The slaves' lives were not their own. Some slaves were brave enough and lucky enough to escape to freedom. They were known as **fugitive** (**few** ja tiv, runaway) slaves. Some fugitive slaves came to Wisconsin, where slavery was **illegal,** or not allowed by law. They **smuggled** themselves (illegally traveled) across the Illinois border or along the Mississippi River shore. Some stayed in Wisconsin. Others ran farther north, all the way to Canada.

After the Civil War, two former slaves, George and Mary Sublett, lived on a small farm in Racine. They were free, but that freedom had cost them almost everything. As an old man, George wrote down their story

"I was born a slave," George wrote, "but I could not silence the enchanting voice . . . telling me of Freedom." As a slave, George's name was Nash Bird. He dreamed of freedom. He longed for freedom. But he loved his wife, Mary, and their children even more than freedom. His owner had promised that the family would never be sold and separated, so Nash Bird pushed away those dreams of freedom.

Sometimes a drawing of a runaway slave like this would appear on a reward poster.

$100 REWARD.

Ran away from my farm, near Buena Vista P. O., Prince George's County, Maryland, on the first day of April, 1855, my servant MATHEW TURNER.

He is about five feet six or eight inches high; weighs from one hundred and sixty to one hundred and eighty pounds; he is very black, and has a remarkably thick upper lip and neck; looks as if his eyes are half closed; walks slow, and talks and laughs loud.

I will give One Hundred Dollars reward to whoever will secure him in jail, so that I get him again, no matter where taken.

MARCUS DU VAL.

BUENA VISTA P. O., MD.,
MAY 10, 1855.

This is one example of a reward poster for a runaway slave. Who was the slave? Who was the owner?

George wrote, "It was in September 1847 as I was returning from the city with the **Madame** [female slave owner], being her coachman. I met a **Negro** [**nee** grow, African American] trader taking away my oldest girl—my loving Harriet. The silence of Death came between us. . . . I knew she had been sold and was going I knew not where. The next day our owner took our oldest boy to the same trader and sold him."

Imagine! First Harriet was taken. Then Nash and Mary's son. Where had they gone? Only the slave owner or the slave trader knew. Nash had believed that his family wouldn't be sold, but now he could never trust his master again.

George wrote, "From that hour I was exploring the territory of the U.G.R.R." George meant the Underground Railroad, a secret organization that helped African Americans escape slavery. With a few dollars and the promise of help from a free black friend, Nash and Mary Bird took their three remaining children and ran. They crossed the Mississippi River at night. "Like criminals we laid by all the second day and at dark started again," George wrote. So they ran, hiding by day and moving at night. Their owner offered a $500 reward for

Slave States, Free States, and Underground Railroad Routes

WISCONSIN

This map shows slave states, free states, and some Underground Railroad routes to the North. Some slaves escaped to ships on the Great Lakes and sailed on to Canada, where slavery was not allowed.

N
W—E
S

Free states
Slave states
Territories
1860 state boundaries
Underground Railroad

Map by Amelia Janes/Mike Gallagher, Midwest Educational Graphics

their capture. Slave catchers and bloodhounds sniffed at their trail. Every day the danger grew.

They were desperate. A white man claimed that he worked with the Underground Railroad. He offered to help Nash and Mary, so they followed him. But early one evening, the man gave a signal, and, in an instant, eight club-carrying slave catchers ran from the woods. The family was surrounded. They had been tricked!

26

Bad turned to worse. Mary and the children were taken away. Nash escaped, but he couldn't find his wife and children. Wild with fear, he hunted everywhere. He did not know what happened to them. Days passed without a single sign of his family. Later he learned that Mary and the baby were sold to one buyer. The other two children—just five and six years old—were sold to another buyer. Nash searched, but he found none of them.

The Underground Railroad helped Nash Bird reach Wisconsin. Once here, he changed his name to George Sublett. He **grieved** (greevd, was deeply sad). Mary was in Louisiana, trapped in slavery. She was sold again and again. "Years had passed," George wrote, "and a rumor came. Mary was dead. Almost I felt my heart grow lighter, for she was no longer a slave!"

George believed the rumor that Mary was dead, but he was determined to save his children. Twice he crossed the Mississippi River to the slave state of Missouri. Leaky boats, mosquitoes, and even the sight of his former owner didn't stop George. He found his son. Then he smuggled his daughter Jane from St. Louis in the dark of night, carrying her baby for twelve miles.

George had found some happiness. At least he had his son and daughter. Then in 1860 his world turned upside down. The rumor about Mary's death proved untrue.

Fugitive slaves used this tunnel at the Milton House Hotel in Milton as a place to hide. The Milton House was a stop on the Underground Railroad from the 1840s to the 1860s. The tunnel allowed people to enter and leave the hotel basement without being seen, since it connected the hotel to an outlying cabin.

Somehow Mary escaped. She came North and found him. Imagine! For so many years he had cried for Mary. Suddenly everything changed. She was alive, and their family was together!

The Civil War began in 1861. George and Mary Sublett traveled to Missouri again, hoping to find their other children. This time—the third time George had traveled to Missouri to find one of his children—he went as a free man. He wrote, "Again we left St. Louis. The 3rd time I had left the city with some freed one of my family. We no longer needed the cover of darkness to hide us . . . but in open day-light we could go like others aboard a handsome boat and like others take seats in the rear of the overland railroad." They found one son in the Union army.

Illustration by Susan Manske

Think how quiet Jane's baby had to be as George Sublett smuggled them out of St. Louis in the middle of the night!

For the rest of their lives, Mary and George Sublett lived in Racine. George sold vegetables and did odd jobs. Mary took in laundry and cleaned. Few people knew how their kind, hard-working old neighbors had suffered for freedom. Few people realized the strength and bravery the Subletts had shown in helping their family reach Wisconsin.

Looking Back, Looking Forward

The Nattestad, Kazmerchak, Dudden, and Kanter families all lived in poverty. Even with hard work they couldn't own the land they farmed or the houses they lived in. Like so many others, they decided to leave because of opportunities in a new place

and because of hardship, hunger, and injustice in their old homes. They turned dreams into action, came to the United States, and settled in Wisconsin.

Poverty, hardship, and injustice were not just the experiences of Norwegians, Prussians, Russian Jews, or Irish people. American sharecroppers also hoped for fair pay and better opportunities. Those hopes brought many sharecroppers and their families, like Rubie Bond's, to Wisconsin.

Today, many farm workers still try to escape poverty by finding new homes. **Migrant** (**my** grant) workers often travel north from South Texas, Mexico, and Central America, picking whatever crop is in season. They, too, work on someone else's land. Some pick crops in Wisconsin: cherries, potatoes, and cranberries. Many decide to stay and make Wisconsin their home.

In "A Closer Look," you read the Sublett story. You know about George's many journeys to gather the family together in Wisconsin. In the next unit, you'll learn more about different kinds of journeys.

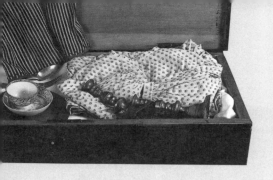

Unit 2
Making the Journey

These are the kinds of stories you'll read about in this unit.

 Packing Up

 Many Kinds of Journeys

 DANGER!

 New Life, New Problems

You might be going to school for the day, to a friend's overnight, or to your grandmother's for the weekend. Wherever you're going, you have to plan ahead. First you try to imagine what activities you will be doing. Then you pack your backpack or suitcase with the things you'll need.

What if you knew that you were not returning home? What if, instead of a day or a night or a weekend, you'd be traveling for many weeks or months to a new home? You would have so much to think about: how you would be traveling, what you might need to eat and wear during your journey, and what you would need when you arrived at your **destination** (des tuh **na** shun, journey's end).

TIMELINE

These are the people you will meet in this unit, and these are the dates when they were making their journeys to Wisconsin.

1842
Oswald Ragatz; Ole and Ansten Nattestad; Michael Brady
▼

1848
Clara Brauns; John Frederick Diederichs
▼

1840			1850

▲
1847
John Greening

▲
1849
John Muir

30

Maybe you've moved from some other part of town, or from another community, state, or country to where you live now. If so, you know how difficult it is to decide what you must bring along and what you must leave behind.

This unit contains many stories about the journeys people made to reach Wisconsin. You'll find very different answers to each of the following questions: What supplies did people pack for their journeys? How did they travel to Wisconsin? What dangers did people face as they traveled? And finally, what new problems and difficulties did these immigrants and migrants meet and deal with along the way? Even though some people made their journeys more than one hundred years ago, do any of the problems sound familiar today?

1891–1892
Kanter Family

1979–1998
Maria Covarrubias

1890   1900   1910   1920   1970   1980   1990

1917
Rubie Bond

Packing Up

Everyone dreams. Many people chase after those dreams. But only a brave and lucky few ever catch them. It is one thing to sit around the fire on a cozy winter evening dreaming of America. It is another thing to sell everything and spend all your money on steamship tickets.

It is one thing for people like the Kazmerchak or Nattestad brothers, the Kanters, or the Bonds to dream of leaving the place they've always lived. It's another thing to make plans, sell things that can't be moved, and pack the rest.

Anyone can dream. It takes real courage to make dreams come true. The people who came to Wisconsin had that courage.

Illustration by Jill Bremigan

32

Leaving Switzerland

As an older man, Oswald Ragatz told the story of his family's decision to move from Tamins, Switzerland, to Sauk City in 1842. In all, eleven people came. First, his oldest brother, Christian, was sent ahead to find a place to live. Back in Switzerland, the family waited. Months passed.

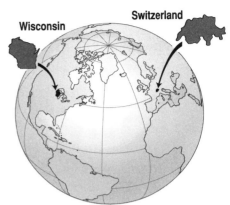

Wisconsin

Switzerland

Map by Amelia Janes/Mike Gallagher,
Midwest Educational Graphics

"Father was strangely silent," Oswald wrote. "Mother often wept. But, at length, a long letter came." Christian wrote of good land and rich soil in Wisconsin. Christian's letter sounded promising. With that bit of hope, the family made their plans to journey to America.

WHS Archives, Name File

Oswald Ragatz as an adult, long after his adventurous trip to America.

Oswald thought the trip to America would be an adventure. Talk of danger just made him more excited. "I felt very important," he remembered years later. "[I] told my **envious** [**en** vee us, jealous] companions that I would shoot a lion for each of them immediately upon my arrival. What is more, I really believed so!"

First, Oswald's father sold their mill and house. Second, chairs and clocks, animals and farm equipment were sold off. Finally, father, mother, children, and trunks were piled into a wagon. The family headed west. Mile after mile, they drove until they reached France, where the ship waited to take them to America. That was just the beginning. You'll find out much more about their journey later in this unit.

Starting Out on Skis

Remember Ole and Ansten Nattestad, the brothers from Norway who had caught America Fever in 1842? They needed to come up with money for their journey. They emptied their bank accounts. When their last silver **kroner** (Norwegian money) was counted, they had enough to equal 200 U.S. dollars. It was enough—but barely enough—for steamship tickets and food.

Reaching the sailing ship was a problem for the Nattestad brothers. Two hundred miles of mountains stretched between their little village and the harbor in Stavanger. How were they to get there? They had sold their horses. Trains couldn't cross those steep mountains. It cost too much to rent a stagecoach. Ole and Ansten had to save their money for crossing the Atlantic Ocean. But they were determined to reach America.

How would you like to pack everything you needed for a journey to America in a backpack and start out on skis? Would it be fun? Scary? Both?

"Our equipment consisted of the clothes we wore, a pair of skis, and a knapsack," Ole wrote. "People looked at us in wonder . . . we must have lost our senses." Ole and Ansten tossed those knapsacks over their shoulders and started for America on skis!

When the Nattestads reached America, they still had eighty dollars. That's not much money to start a new life. But it was enough to get them to Wisconsin.

34

Goodbye to Grandpa

Have you heard of John Muir, the inventor, writer, and nature lover? Today, nature centers, schools, and parks are named for him. Long before he was famous in Wisconsin, he was a small boy in Dunbar, Scotland, who

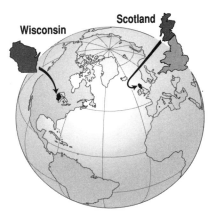

Map by Amelia Janes/Mike Gallagher,
Midwest Educational Graphics

liked playing more than working at home or in school. He loved to wrestle with his brothers, hurl stones into the duck pond, and run like a wild pony across his father's fields.

John Muir as a young man in 1863, fourteen years after he arrived in Wisconsin.

All that changed with one decision. One spring night in 1849, John Muir's father, a stern, unsmiling man, announced to the family after supper, "Tomorrow we go to America."

The family was stunned. America? Tomorrow? John wanted to cheer. Going to America in the morning meant *no school!* He imagined himself fishing in the rivers and hunting in the woods. He would have adventures! As he opened his mouth to shout, John felt his grandfather's arms around him. The old man was weeping. Then John understood that going to America also meant leaving his grandpa behind.

This house was one of John Muir's childhood homes in Portage, but it wasn't the first place his family lived after they arrived.

Guidebooks and Goodbyes

Making the decision to leave for America was hard for everyone. Even people who lived with poverty and persecution made the decision with hearts heavy with sadness. Preparing to leave was even harder. Families sold their farms, land, houses, and milk cows. Children watched as strangers paid for and carried away belongings like Mama's special rocking chair or Papa's plow.

Some **emigrants** (**em** mi grants, people who leave one country to move to another) were lucky to escape with a little money and a bundle of clothes. Some were able to plan and save money for the long trip across the ocean. Guidebooks for emigrants were written in many languages. In 1853, Christian Ficker wrote a guidebook in German that included grocery lists, prices of everything from tickets to steamer trunks, and warnings about thieves, cheats, and "scalawags" (scal uh wags, dishonest people).

Ficker's guidebook had plenty of advice. "Lock everything with real door locks in waterproof chests." Immigrants must bring food enough for the journey across the ocean, things like "wine, rum, dried fruit, smoked sausages and ham, well-baked **zwiebach** [**zwy** bock, very dry toast] . . . butter . . . cheese, pickles . . . salt, pepper, some vinegar . . . oat grits for **vomiting** [**vom** it ing, throwing up] and seasickness, coffee, woolen blankets, and mattresses stuffed with seaweed."

Other guidebooks warned sea travelers to bring their own water, dried beans or peas, salted herring, and oatmeal to fill their stomachs when the good food rotted or ran out.

Freundlicher Rathgeber

für Alle,

welche nach **Amerika** und vorzugsweise

nach

Wisconsin

auswandern wollen.

Von

Christian Traugott Ficker,

Farmer in Mequon, Wisconsin, Nord-Amerika,
früher Cantor und Knabenlehrer in Staucha bei Lommatzsch
im Königreich Sachsen.

Leipzig, 1853.
J. G. Mittler.

This is a photograph of Ficker's German guidebook, used by emigrants to help them prepare for their journey to America and then Wisconsin. Can you find the date it was printed? In what German city was it printed?

Christian Traugott Ficker, *Freundlicher Rathgeber*, WHS Rare Books Collection

In the end, most people filled travel trunks with items they believed would be hard to replace in America. "Be sure to bring your tools," wrote one immigrant to his brother. "Good, warm stockings," wrote another. Some women were afraid America would be an endless wilderness where they would never be able to buy proper, "ladylike" clothes.

Carpenter Henrey Brandes, Sr., brought these tools with him from Germany to Bridgeport around 1846. You can see them in an exhibit at the Wisconsin Historical Museum.
All photos this page by Joel Heiman

They packed **corsets** (stiff underwear designed to give women smaller waists), hats, petticoats, shawls, and yards and yards of cloth to make clothing.

Immigrants' travel trunks and suitcases held memories, too. Special objects like Grandma's silver candlesticks, family pictures, or great-grandfather's pocket watch were keepsakes that people saved to remember loved ones left behind.

When the last piece of furniture was sold, every trunk was stuffed with clothes, tools, and important keepsakes, and the tickets were bought, it was finally time to leave. Time to say goodbye. One last hug. One last tear. One final promise not to forget those left behind.

In 1836, James Weaver brought these candlesticks from Sussex, England, to Sussex, Wisconsin. It seems that he or someone from his hometown carried the town's name with them when emigrating!

Waiting to Go

Once people decided to go to America, some were able to leave quickly. Others had to save and plan carefully. Still others, like Azriel and Rosa Kanter, wanted to leave but had no money.

Jews in Europe knew about the suffering of Russia's Jews. They donated money for tickets to America. Chief **Rabbi** (**rab** by, Jewish teacher and leader) Furmanski organized a committee to make sure that money went to honest Jews who needed help. Azriel Kanter heard this. Finally, a spark of hope! He was a good citizen and a faithful Jew. Could he escape with his family?

Azriel and Rosa decided to try. But first, they needed travel papers from the Russian government. They sold everything, and Azriel went to the city. He filled out paper after paper to apply for **passports** (official travel papers). Then he waited. And waited. And waited.

"Still no word," he wrote in his diary, ". . . and no way to earn a **kopek** [**ko** pek, small coin]. All I can do is sit and eat. God forbid that the authorization might not come. Where would I go then?"

Azriel waited for weeks. "I can't leave here," he wrote. "I don't have my papers. To start out on an overseas journey with the family is impossible! To go without the family is no good either." Finally, he decided there was no choice but to buy false passports.

Two months later, with his money nearly gone, Azriel's situation became even darker. His wallet was stolen. Everything—every official paper, including his birth certificate—was gone!

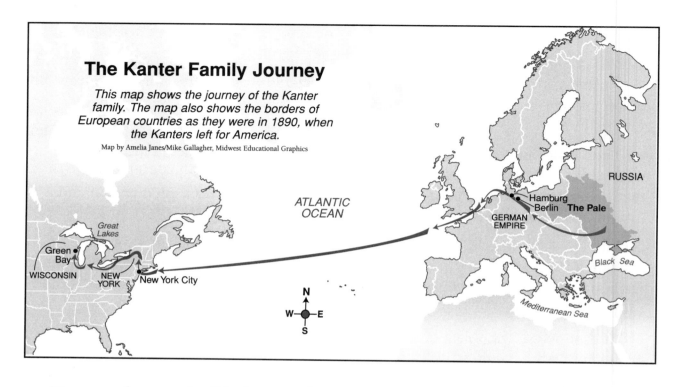

The Kanter Family Journey

This map shows the journey of the Kanter family. The map also shows the borders of European countries as they were in 1890, when the Kanters left for America.

Map by Amelia Janes/Mike Gallagher, Midwest Educational Graphics

RUSSIA

Hamburg
Berlin **The Pale**

GERMAN
EMPIRE

ATLANTIC
OCEAN

Great
Lakes

Green
Bay

WISCONSIN

NEW
YORK

New York City

Black Sea

Mediterranean Sea

N
W—E
S

He wrote desperately, "Nothing to show, nothing at all! I lie here feeling as if my hair is on fire. I am hiding in my room, afraid to go out into the street."

Finally, Azriel begged for help. Some friends wrote Rabbi Furmanski, saying Azriel was a faithful Jew. By then, however, so much time had passed that the money for tickets to America was nearly gone. Finally, Azriel's uncle tried a trick common in Russia—bribery! He offered money to the government officials for false travel papers.

It worked. Azriel and Rosa received the false papers, and they hurried to get their ticket money. At Rabbi Furmanski's home, they found a mob scene.

"Hundreds were crowded in front of Furmanski's gate and were practically thrown off the steps. I was one of the lucky ones," Azriel wrote. Quickly, they gathered their children and a few belongings.

They made one last visit to their families. They stayed with family for fourteen days. Rosa and Azriel held their old parents' hands, knowing they would never see them again. Sadness was like a heavy weight. Azriel wrote about his sorrow in his diary. "Who could describe this family's feelings? There is no need to; we can all imagine them. . . . My heart felt so . . . that I could barely breathe."

"At our departure there was again a scene of wailing and weeping and enough tears to form a small lake." In the winter cold, Azriel and Rosa walked to the border, carrying the children in their arms.

At each town, the police questioned the family. They examined every paper and dug through every suitcase. Azriel and Rosa lived in fear. "Once they start poking into the records and discover I have a false passport, and that I never registered for [the army], I am lost for good," Azriel worried. But, miraculously, they weren't discovered.

The Kanters' travel papers listed false names, because the Russian government kept Jews from leaving. Azriel's papers said he was a businessman traveling to Germany with his family. "I received a certificate under the name of Yossel Itzik Horowitz, and that is the name I took."

"Russian scoundrels," Azriel complained. "They drive the Jews out and then don't let them leave!"

After many frightening days, the Kanters finally bribed the border guards and crossed into Germany. Azriel could hardly find the words to write down his feelings. "We were overjoyed at being out of Russia, not quaking at every sound, afraid of every fly. It was like being in the dark and then coming into broad daylight. How bright everything looked!"

The Kanters hoped that the police would not guess that their papers were false.

Rosa and Azriel still had so many miles to travel. Many policemen and government officials would look at their papers and ask the same, worrisome questions. Did they have permission to leave Russia? Were they criminals? Did they have all the correct papers?

Each day they traveled. Each night they slept in a different city. Their money was quickly disappearing. One night, they were told about a free immigrant shelter. They carried the children and their suitcase and walked block after block to this place. "It was bitterly cold. . . ." Azriel wrote. "The children whimpered . . . and were beginning to feel heavy. . . .We finally reached our **sanctuary** [**sanc** chu air ee, a safe place]—and . . . what did we find? A roomful of poor wretches, beggars. . . . How can anyone stay here? There are no beds; just sacks of straw on the floor." Azriel thought, "How can anyone even think of spending the night here?" Yet, they did stay. They had no choice. "Rosa and I ate nothing. The children took a few spoons of soup and a bit of meat."

The next day the weary family stumbled onto a train to Berlin. Their journey was almost over. They clung to each other and to the hope of America.

The train was crammed door-to-door with three hundred Russian **refugees** (**ref** yu jeez, people forced to leave home because of war or disaster). "We had to get the baggage and the children into the railroad car. We climb in . . . there is a terrible crush; people pushing and . . . scrambling madly with bags and baggage. . . . Women are screaming, children wailing, and the air is full of shouts. . . . There is no water in the car. . . . One way or another we managed until the second night when the train pulled into . . . Berlin."

A surprise waited in Berlin. A wealthy Jewish family had opened their home to all three hundred refugees. Hot food! Warm blankets! The family gave money to people who had spent their last coins. The kindness brought tears to Rosa's eyes.

✈ Many Kinds of Journeys

When you hear the word *immigrant,* do you imagine a ship with cloud-white sails and sunlight sparkling on a calm, blue ocean? Or does a picture of children peeking around a canvas-covered wagon pop into your mind? Have you seen old black and white photos of Ellis Island in New York Harbor? From 1897 to 1938, millions of immigrants entered the United States there. If you have seen any of those old photos, you might think of a tired-looking grandma in a headscarf or a man bending under the weight of a trunk tied with rope.

After arriving in the United States, people traveled to Wisconsin by land or by water. Both immigrants from other countries and settlers from eastern states bumped and swayed along dirt roads in covered or open wagons. Some crossed the Great Lakes by steamship. In the 1850s, some rode fancy new steam-engine trains. Others,

Some people came to Wisconsin by wagon, like these settlers who arrived in Poynette in the late 1870s. Look what they brought with them—horses and cows!

like the Mohican Indians, came by the only means they could afford—by oxcart and on foot.

People often traveled from New York to Wisconsin through the Great Lakes. What a trip! Immigrants and others who came from New York City hired wagons or took boats up the Hudson River to reach the Erie Canal. Then they traveled by canal boat or train to Lake Erie. From there steamships took them across the Great Lakes. Steamers were a cheap way to travel, but they were also uncomfortable, filthy, and dangerous.

Later, in the twentieth century, people more often made their way to Wisconsin by train, car, and even later, by airplane.

Crossing the Atlantic

Millions of people from Europe reached the United States by crossing the Atlantic Ocean. At first ships were powered by wind and sail. Pictures of sailing ships that crossed the ocean in the 1800s look beautiful. In reality, they were often crowded, stinking, and dangerous. The trip across the Atlantic usually took five to eight weeks! Of course, storms, bad winds, or no wind at all sometimes meant immigrants spent eight, nine, or even more weeks

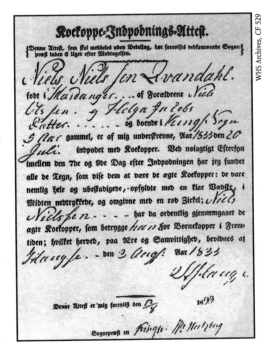

WHS Archives, CF 529

All immigrants had to be prepared for a health check when they arrived in the United States. This is the vaccination certificate of a Norwegian immigrant, dated 1833. Can you find his name?

on board these cramped and uncomfortable ships. Without wind, a ship could sit for days without moving a single mile.

By the mid-1800s, some people were already crossing the Atlantic by steamship. By the early 1900s, steamships had replaced sailing **vessels** (**ves** suls, boats or ships). Steamships burned coal. In giant boilers, water was heated to make steam. Steam ran the ships' engines. On a good day, a steamer could travel as much as two hundred miles. At that speed, steamers could cross the Atlantic in half the time it took slower sailing ships. Passengers were thrilled, but their journeys could still be difficult.

This drawing of a steamship comes from the diary and sketchbook of John Zeier, who settled in Dane County in the mid-1800s. He traveled on this steamship from Buffalo, New York, to Milwaukee. His diary contains many drawings of his life in Wisconsin between 1847 and 1878.

Life aboard Ship

Travelers filled diaries and letters with stories of these journeys. Some stories were wonderful. Some were terrifying. On March 23, 1842, Michael Brady began a journal of his trip from Ireland to America by writing, "This morning I left my father and mother to go to America to seek my fortune in the name of God." As you will see, his writing reminds us that rules for exact spelling were not in place that long ago.

"Sailed this thirtyeth day of March. Good faire weather up to the 7th of April when we had . . . a severe snow storm." The ship sailed through storm after storm. One storm lasted four days and nights. The wind screamed, and waves rose up like cliffs beside the ship. When the wind howled, the ship rolled and tossed on high, rough waves. Water flooded down the **hatch** (a covered door in the deck of the ship) into the area below deck, called **steerage** (**steer** idg).

Only the poorest people stayed in steerage. It was crowded. Bunk beds lined the walls. Whenever the ship rolled, people, cooking pots, and anything not tied down flew across the room. During a storm, people were so seasick they thought they were going to die. Worried parents clung to their children and prayed.

WHS Archives, CF 529

Life in steerage was really awful. Poor, sick, and tired people were crammed into a dark, cramped, and smelly space below deck.

What a storm! The main **mast** (the tall pole on the deck of the ship that supports the largest sails) was as big as a tree. When a strong gust of wind hit, the mast snapped like a pencil! A **deckhand** (worker on the ship) was washed overboard!

Brady wrote all about that storm in his journal. During his journey, he also added many details about other storms, sharks, icebergs, leaking water barrels, and even fights between passengers.

Traveling in steerage meant wall-to-wall people sleeping two or three to a

Even today October is a dangerous month for sea travel, when hurricanes are very common.

bunk. There was little fresh air. The whole place smelled like sweat, vomit, and yesterday's supper. Barrels of fresh drinking water were too precious to be wasted for washing, so people bathed in salty seawater. Soon, saltwater gave them skin rashes. They scratched and complained from morning until night. With people living so close together, germs spread easily, sometimes causing deadly infections.

Even everyday chores like cooking were difficult on board a sailing ship. Michael Brady wrote about the simple job of getting breakfast. "I went out to cook breakfast. My **spider** [cooking pot] was upset and spilt . . . all fifteen eggs with two **lbs.** [pounds] of good Irish bacon. And as I was standing looking most **grevious** [grievous, **gree** vus, very upset] . . . the waves washed overboard and wet me all over. As I was hurrying down to the steerage I slipt going down stairs and fell into a pot of **stirribout** [oatmeal]! You may guess how I felt after all that got threw [through]."

Sharks, Whales, and Weevils

You met the Ragatz family at the beginning of this unit, as they packed up and left their home in Switzerland and started out for France. When the family reached the city of Paris, France, Oswald Ragatz remembered, "The city was full of soldiers and we saw the fat, jolly king driving through the streets. I was disappointed because he wore no crown, but father said he must have left it at home."

48

Then the Ragatz family headed to the harbor city of Havre (**ahv** ruh), where their ship, the *Wood Leid,* was waiting. Oswald was so excited, he ran up and down the docks and climbed on the piles of luggage.

Oswald loved the ship. For him, every day was an adventure. Sailors climbed along the rigging high above the deck. In good weather, passengers played the fiddle and danced. In bad weather, anything could happen. One storm ripped the mast off and smashed the upper deck into a pile of kindling wood.

Illustration by Susan Manske

Oswald climbed up the piles of luggage when he and his family were waiting to board the Wood Leid.

In Switzerland, Oswald's whole world had been a small village. On the ocean, his world opened like a window. He saw amazing things and met amazing people. In Switzerland, he'd only heard of African people, but on the *Wood Leid,* he met Moses, a kind black man who taught him English and sang hymns. Oswald explored the whole ship, climbing down into steerage to make friends with the children and coming back, smiling, happy, but infested with lice. His mother said there would be no more playing in steerage!

Oswald wrote, "There were many chickens, some pigs, and sheep . . . and a cow aboard. . . . We children made pets . . . even of the **swine** [pigs]. . . . Father bought some fresh **mutton** [lamb] from the cook once. It tasted delicious, even if we had played with the poor sheep the day before."

The ship headed south, toward Africa, and across the Atlantic Ocean. Oswald wanted to see everything. Flying fish! Whales! He wrote, "We saw . . . sharks. . . . It gave one a creepy feeling to see their . . . fins cutting the surface of the water. . . . We saw a huge turtle, too, as big as a table top."

Oswald thought that the sailors were amazing, too. One hot day, some sailors dove overboard for a swim. Oswald was wishing he could dive in, too, when he heard a scream. A shark had attacked one of the sailors. The other sailors shouted and raced for the boat and hauled the wounded man up by a rope. The shark had bitten a chunk right out of his shoulder!

Oswald couldn't believe what happened next. "What do you suppose he [the wounded sailor] had come aboard for? A knife! And, with a long, sharp one between his teeth, he jumped overboard again . . . he was more concerned over not being able to fight the fish than over his wound."

Crossing the Atlantic took a long time. On days without wind, the ship sat still as a stone. A passenger died. The captain and crew were young and had little experience. Oswald remembered this awful time. "The water supply ran low. What little remained was so **foul** [rotten] that it stank. . . . Several of the passengers now ran out of food. . . . They had to be fed by the rest of us. . . . The bacon was covered with mould and had to be boiled. The meal was full of **weevils** [little bugs]. When one man complained, the captain growled, 'You ought to appreciate the beetles—they're meat and are thrown in free.'"

Finally, the ship entered the Gulf of Mexico. Every day seemed hotter than the one before. Then at last the *Wood Leid* reached America. They were sailing up the Mississippi River to New Orleans. Oswald wrote, "After sixty-one **interminable** [in **tur** min ubl, endless] days on the wide ocean, the watchman . . . shouted, 'Land! America!!' Everyone strained his eyes and . . . sure enough, a faint line of blue appeared on the horizon. Land, solid land again!" Land! No more thirsty days or hungry nights. No more storms or moldy bacon! The passengers hugged the railing and cheered.

Overboard!

John Greening and his family traveled to Black Earth from England in 1847. The Greenings boarded the sailing ship *Radius* in Liverpool, England, with tickets to America in hand. Soon they heard arguing and shouting. The owners had sold too many tickets. There were thirty-six more people than the ship could carry. As more and more passengers arrived waving their tickets, the captain panicked. The ship couldn't hold any more weight. No captain

Map by Amelia Janes/Mike Gallagher, Midwest Educational Graphics

in his right mind would take the risk. He ordered the crew to cast off, leaving the passengers, with tickets already purchased, red-faced and angry on the docks.

As the boat pulled away, the captain counted passengers. The number was still too high. He ordered the last twelve people who had arrived to be sent back. Those passengers argued and cried, but nothing would change the captain's mind. The awful scene stuck in John's mind:

"The sea ran so high that the steamer refused to come alongside . . . to take them out and our captain said he would throw them overboard. . . . So the poor **wretches** [**ret** chez; very sad people] were dragged from their **berths** [bunks below deck] and lowered to a boat . . . the sea breaking over them."

The passengers huddled in the little boat as their luggage was piled in a huge net. Sailors slowly lowered the swaying, heavy bundle down from the *Radius* toward the smaller boat. With every minute, the sea became rougher. The *Radius* bounced up and down in the waves. The small boat rolled from side to side. Icy water wet the passengers to the skin. The captain roared orders. Then, in an instant, the net swung wide and the rope snapped, hurling every single piece of luggage into the water. John Greening was horrified, but the captain didn't seem bothered at all. And twelve people had just seen everything they owned sink to the bottom of Liverpool Harbor!

Drawing by Middleton High School student Marieka Brouwer

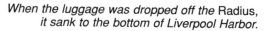
When the luggage was dropped off the Radius, *it sank to the bottom of Liverpool Harbor.*

From Hamburg to New York

Remember Azriel and Rosa Kanter's long, hard journey from Russia to Germany? The kindness they received in Berlin helped them reach the harbor in Hamburg. Azriel, Rosa, and their children boarded a steamship there and began the last part of their weary journey. The ship was crowded. The food was bad. Passengers were unable to leave their bunks, they were so seasick. But none of that mattered. They were going to America at last.

Azriel and Rosa hung on to the hope of America every day for seven long weeks until their ship entered New York Harbor. Later, Azriel remembered every moment. "Everybody was overjoyed!" he wrote. "Tomorrow we were entering New York City! Hardly anyone slept that night. . . . We scrubbed and washed and unpacked our best clothes in honor of the Golden Land."

Illustration by Jill Bremigan

Azriel, Rosa, Cele, and Ellie stood on the deck of the ship and cheered. "Long live America! Long live America!" It was April 1892 when Azriel, Rosa, Cele, and Ellie Kanter arrived in New York City.

⚠ DANGER!

Some journeys were filled with events and adventures that were even scarier than storms and sharks. Often people faced dangers that threatened their lives. Some travelers never reached their destinations.

Great Lakes Pirates

In 1848, a little German girl named Clara Brauns (**brawnz**) came across the Great Lakes on a sailing **schooner** (**skoo** nur, a type of sailboat widely used in the Great Lakes) to settle with her family in Green Bay. Years and years later, when Clara was an eighty-eight-year-old grandma, she still remembered that trip.

Clara was aboard the schooner when it hit a sandbar. Then the wind disappeared for days and fog settled around the ship, making it impossible even

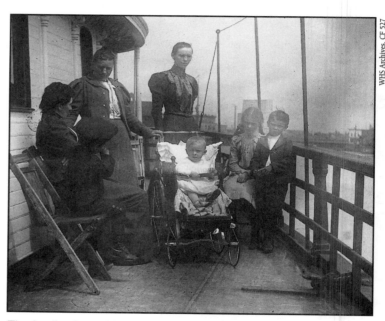

The family pictured here traveled on a Great Lakes steamer, just like John Greening and Clara Brauns. This photograph was taken aboard the Sheboygan *in 1899.*

to see the shore. She wrote that "there was a strange looking vessel lying quite still in a little bay. . . . The captain did not like the looks of it. . . . There was no sail to be seen, nor smoke . . . when all at once we saw smoke, and in a shorter time than it takes me to tell it, sails went up. The vessel whirled around, headed toward us and sailed along . . . as if it were chasing us. . . . About noon the captain ordered his men to load all the guns."

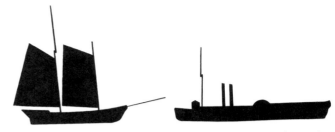

Schooners had sails. Steamers did not have to depend on the wind for power. WHS Underwater Archaeology Program

Pirates! Clara didn't dare even whisper the word. Her heart must have beat like a big bass drum! Sailors said they had heard before of thieves slipping out of hidden harbors to rob immigrant ships. All afternoon the mysterious ship chased them. Clara was terrified.

"Sometimes we sailed so fast that we left the boat far behind. . . . At times it gained on us and came so near we could see it plainly." All night the captain and crew stood guard with their guns loaded. In the morning, the ship was gone.

The dangers on Clara's journey weren't over yet. Near Milwaukee, another storm stirred up. The wind howled. Fog hung along the shore as thick and heavy as a featherbed. Clara hid her face in her mother's skirts. Had they crossed the ocean and escaped pirates only to crash on the rocks?

They couldn't go on, and they couldn't turn around. With the wind behind them and fog and rocks along the shore, the captain didn't dare move an inch closer to land.

"We could see nothing at all." Clara remembered. "Even we children did not go to bed that night. Very late we came to Milwaukee, or near it. We had to go ashore in a small rowboat. . . . It had grown cloudy . . . we heard distant thunder. The lake was getting rough and there was no harbor or pier." Clara, her family, and all the other passengers were rowed to shore and dumped on an empty beach in the fog with their luggage piled beside them.

"Here we were on the beach . . . and the night so dark that we could scarcely see to walk. . . . We children clung shivering to our parents." At least the family had reached Wisconsin alive.

Worrying about Shipwrecks

In 1848, John Frederick Diederichs (**dee** dricks) left Elberfeld, Germany, to **immigrate** (**im** mig grate, arrive to live permanently in another country) to Manitowoc. He wrote about his family's trip by steamboat from Buffalo, New York, to

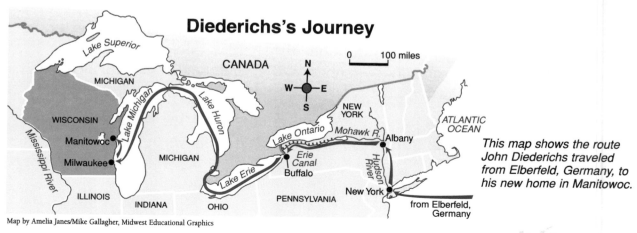

Diederichs's Journey

This map shows the route John Diederichs traveled from Elberfeld, Germany, to his new home in Manitowoc.

Map by Amelia Janes/Mike Gallagher, Midwest Educational Graphics

Milwaukee. "On this trip, which is usually made in 5 or 6 days, we spent 11 days," he wrote, "the hardest and most dangerous part of our journey. Several weeks ago a steamboat [the *Phoenix*, (**fe** nix)] was destroyed by fire near Sheboygan."

DID YOU KNOW?

John Diederichs was right. Travel on the Great Lakes *was* dangerous. Every year ships sank in storms, ran aground in fog, or crashed onto sandbars. Fire was a constant worry. A ship's boiler could explode, gas lamps could tip over, or cookstoves could flame out of control. Many people, like those unlucky people aboard the *Phoenix,* crossed an entire ocean only to drown in Lake Michigan.

Milwaukee Sentinel & Gazette, November 24, 1847

This headline appeared in the Milwaukee Sentinel & Gazette *in its report of the sinking of the* Phoenix.

N. Currier, publisher, n.d.

On April 17, 1845, the steamboat Swallow *was on the way from Albany to New York when it struck a large rock, caught on fire, broke in two, and sank. Great Lakes travel was dangerous!*

New Life, New Problems

Most immigrants survived the ocean crossing, whether they traveled by sailing vessel or steamship. But when their feet touched solid ground again, their journey was far from over. Traveling within the United States brought more new situations and new problems for families like Oswald Ragatz's.

Freedom for Some

Oswald wrote, "And so we arrived at New Orleans. . . . It seemed strange to have firm ground underfoot again and we had difficulty walking at first. Mother laughed when we children said: 'Why, the ground here looks just like in Switzerland.' I suppose we expected everything in the new world to be different."

The grand city of New Orleans was an adventure, too. While they waited for a Mississippi riverboat headed north, the Ragatz family wandered the streets in amazement. Oswald ate frog's legs and snails, juicy melons, and, an American treat, sweet corn!

New Orleans was beautiful. Sunlight sparkled on the river and the smells of French cooking and flowers floated in the air. Oswald ran back and forth, trying to see everything at once. Not everything he saw was pleasant.

Oswald remembered, "We also saw a sight I shall never forget—the slave market where men and women, some in chains, were being sold like cattle. When a dealer approached us . . . to sell us a servant, we, who were from free little Switzerland, turned away in disgust, father using the strongest language I ever heard come from his lips and mother weeping."

The trip up the Mississippi River made them wish they'd stayed in New Orleans. Mosquitoes attacked them. The heat hung in the air like a woolen blanket. Some of the riverboat workers did double-duty; working on the boat all day and stealing from the passengers at night. Oswald's father and brothers had to stand guard to keep their luggage from being dragged off.

Currier & Ives, publisher, 1870

In 1870 the Mississippi River was a busy, important travel route for vessels of all kinds.

As they passed St. Louis, news came that another steamship, carrying friends from the *Wood Leid,* had burned when the boiler exploded, killing almost everyone on board. The Ragatz family felt very sad, thinking of those friends who had died.

On the fourth of July, Oswald's family arrived in Galena, Illinois. Like many immigrants, they felt numb and exhausted. They were alone. Most of their money was gone. Somehow,

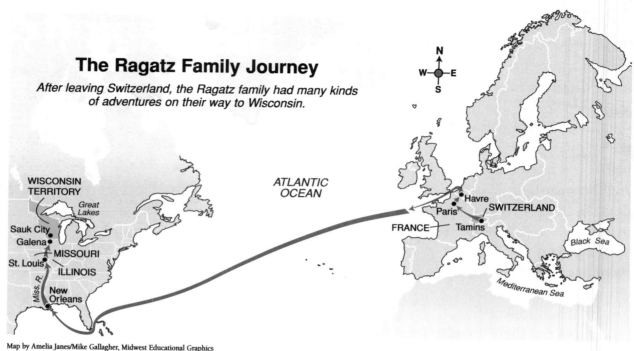

The Ragatz Family Journey

After leaving Switzerland, the Ragatz family had many kinds of adventures on their way to Wisconsin.

Map by Amelia Janes/Mike Gallagher, Midwest Educational Graphics

they had to buy land, learn English, and make a home for themselves. In their hearts, they wondered if leaving Switzerland had been a terrible mistake. There was no turning back. They hung on to hope and to each other and headed for Sauk City.

Getting Cheated

At the docks in New York or New Orleans, immigrants were met by wild confusion. Imagine! Ships, tugboats, and **barges** (flat boats carrying cargo) filled the harbor. People waited on every dock. Trunks and boxes and crates were piled

60

In this drawing of the New Orleans waterfront in 1883, more than thirty steamboats were docked. How many smokestacks can you count? Dockworkers unloaded sugar, cotton, and large amounts of assorted goods, including luggage belonging to people like the Ragatz family. *Frank Leslie's Illustrated Newspaper,* 1883

everywhere. Voices shouted out in different languages. Children cried. Sailors yelled. Horses and wagons crowded the streets.

Agents (people who arrange deals for others) were everywhere. They pounced on the newly arrived immigrants like cats on mice. Immigrants paid agents for help finding temporary rooms, exchanging money for American dollars, and arranging transportation. Some agents were honest. Others were thieves on the lookout for anyone inexperienced, innocent, or unsuspecting.

As trunks and boxes were unloaded from the immigrants' ships, agents hurried over to the newcomers, offering to help. They would offer to carry someone's trunks to a rooming house or find the cheapest tickets to Wisconsin. In an instant, some poor family's luggage would be tossed into the agent's wagon and driven away. *If* the family ever saw their belongings again, they would be forced to pay a huge sum of money just to get them back.

Many immigrants were cheated as they traveled from New York to Wisconsin and other states. John Diederichs, who had written about the burning of the *Phoenix,* warned his friends back in Germany to stay away from agents that he called "sharpers." These agents advertised cheap travel by canalboat. These advertisements were lies. The truth was, the cost for *people* traveling on a canalboat was cheap, but charges for every trunk, box, and parcel were sky-high.

Diederichs wrote a letter to his friends, telling them, "When these sharpers say it is much cheaper to ride on the canal from Albany to Buffalo, they are perfectly right; but . . . they say not a word [about the cost for the luggage]." He warned his friends not to trust advice from any strangers they met.

A Railroad Journey to a New Life

Remember Rubie Bond, who came north from Mississippi in 1917 when she was only ten years old? Like John Muir and Oswald Ragatz, Rubie was excited about her adventure. Years later, she remembered many details about the trip.

"It was hard, leaving the relatives behind, but it was a matter of trying to exist. . . . We took the train from Pontotoc to Beloit. We were just herded onto the train. We paid our own way, I do recall. They had this **Jim Crow** [separate, for African Americans only] section that we rode on until we reached Illinois. . . . Black people always rode in the front coach, up near the engine of the train so they would get all of the soot and dust and what have you. Then, when we reached Illinois, if you wanted to change you could go anyplace on the train.

DID YOU KNOW?

Who Was Jim Crow?

After slavery ended, many white Americans still thought African Americans weren't equal to whites. Both in the South and the North in the late 1800s and early 1900s, laws were passed to keep black people separate from white people. These laws lasted in many places for over fifty years! Some states had separate schools and colleges, separate seats on buses, and even separate restrooms and drinking fountains. Laws that kept black people separate (and unequal) were known as "Jim Crow" laws.

This "Jim Crow" movie theater, shown here in 1944, was in Leland, Mississippi.

"I was ten years old, and moving . . . was just an adventure for me. I remember when the train crossed the Mississippi [River]. In Memphis, Tennessee, there was all this water on each side of the tracks. I remember seeing soldiers—this was the beginning of World War I. It was 1917."

Rubie also remembered the train chugging into Beloit station. And she remembered a strange, new experience in the North—snow!

The name Jim Crow came from a character in American music and dance performances called **minstrel shows.** Many white Americans did not believe African Americans were their equals. But they were **fascinated** (**fas** sin a ted, very curious about) by black culture, especially African American music. In the 1800s and early 1900s, musicians and other entertainers would "black" their faces (put on dark makeup) before performing in minstrel shows. Once in "blackface," these white entertainers copied what *they* believed were black habits. Because the performers often made fun of black people, we now see that minstrel shows were **racist** (treated people unfairly because of their race). Even African American entertainers had to black their faces if they wanted to perform before a white audience.

This 1933 book contained songs, stories, and **skits** (short plays) that made fun of black people and their culture.

A Closer Look

Crossing the Border

In Unit 1, you got to know the Subletts, who arrived in Wisconsin in the late 1840s. They escaped slavery. Nearly 150 years later, Maria and Ismael Covarrubias (mah **ree** ah and iss **mah** el co vah **ru** bee us) also escaped to Wisconsin. In 1979 they left behind poverty in Mexico and later gang violence in Chicago. This is Maria's story of her family's difficult journey.

Maria was a teenager when her story began in Mexico. "I was just 17 when I married. That is our culture: to marry young. The next year the first baby came. Ismael, my husband, lost his job, soon our savings were gone. . . . No one would hire a married woman . . . it is our culture."

Maria and Ismael sold their furniture to pay bills, but Ismael could find no work. Maria's mother had already immigrated to Los Angeles, California. She wrote that jobs were waiting on the other side of the border.

Crossing the border without permission was illegal. People were often caught and put in jail. Maria and Ismael were good people who had never broken laws. Still, they were desperate. They had to find a way to feed their family. Maria and Ismael had heard stories of dangerous border crossings, but had no idea about *how* dangerous. "My Cinthya was just five months old, and crossing [the border] is so much more risky for women and children," Maria said.

Maria and Ismael made a plan. First they traveled from Guadalajara (gwah da la **ha** ra) to Tijuana (tee **whah** na) in Baja (**bah** hah) California, at the border between

The map in the upper left shows Wisconsin and Mexico highlighted.

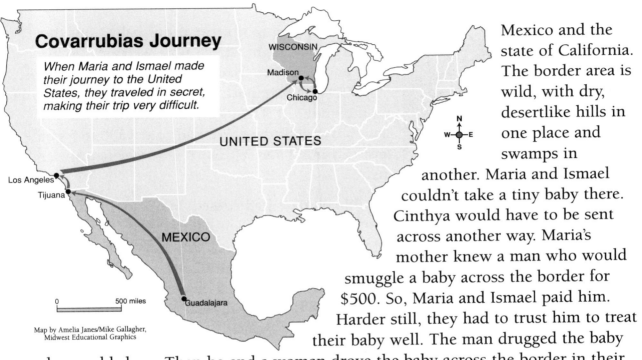

Covarrubias Journey

When Maria and Ismael made their journey to the United States, they traveled in secret, making their trip very difficult.

WISCONSIN

Madison

Chicago

UNITED STATES

N
W — E
S

Los Angeles

Tijuana

MEXICO

0   500 miles

Guadalajara

Map by Amelia Janes/Mike Gallagher,
Midwest Educational Graphics

Mexico and the state of California. The border area is wild, with dry, desertlike hills in one place and swamps in another. Maria and Ismael couldn't take a tiny baby there. Cinthya would have to be sent across another way. Maria's mother knew a man who would smuggle a baby across the border for $500. So, Maria and Ismael paid him. Harder still, they had to trust him to treat their baby well. The man drugged the baby so she would sleep. Then he and a woman drove the baby across the border in their car, as if she was their own child.

That same night, Maria and Ismael tried to cross, as well. But the border police found them in San Isidro, California. Maria remembers that the police were "very violent. . . . They yelled. . . . They . . . took us to prison. Then at 2:30, 3:00 in the morning they took us over to the border and threw us across."

Maria and Ismael were on the Mexican side of the border. Cinthya was on the other side, already in the United States on her way to Maria's mother. Maria said, "We

This photograph of the Covarrubias family was taken in 1987. Ismael and Maria are surrounded by their children. From left to right, the kids are Daniel, Hector, Julie, Cinthya, and Jorge.

had to keep trying [to reach] our baby." But they kept getting caught. "Each time we paid a guide. Paid and paid. We tried to go through the swamps. . . . We were barefoot . . . our shoes were sucked off in the mud. . . . Then we crawled two miles. My knees were bleeding. We had paid $300 to a guide, but he ran off and left us. The border patrol caught us."

Fifteen days had passed. Maria and Ismael's money was gone. Their baby was in Los Angeles. Maria wanted to go back to Guadalajara, but back to what? No furniture, no jobs, no future. Another guide promised to get them safely to Los Angeles for $1,000. In desperation, they borrowed the money from Maria's brothers.

"Seven times in fifteen days we tried. Night after night. We would try one more time." So, thirteen men and one woman, Maria, crossed into California. They kept on the move all night. Maria will never forget that journey.

"Walking, crawling. Under rainwater tunnels, running across highways. . . . We finally got to L.A., and we had no shoes. We were scratched and beaten up. I . . . was so afraid. It was six months before I would leave that house . . . afraid to hear anyone speaking English. Afraid they would know."

In Los Angeles, Maria and Ismael had more babies. They worked and saved. They paid back Maria's brothers. Maria sewed. She picked zucchini, leaving the children with a neighbor. She bent over all day in the fields, working for $1.10 an hour. "In Mexico [people told us] the good, not the truth," Maria said. "They didn't say we would not be wanted or appreciated."

Maria felt the sting of hate and **discrimination** (dis crim ih **na** shun), when people treated her unfairly because she was a Mexican. She worked long hours for low pay. No one seemed to care. Maria explained. "[People say], 'You're coming here to take our jobs.' Not true. People don't want those jobs. . . . They pay us cheap."

In Los Angeles, Maria and Ismael worked hard, but they couldn't get ahead. All their earnings went to rent and food. Another baby was on the way. The little family moved first to Chicago and then to Madison where one of Maria's brothers lived.

"In Madison was the first time I saw snow," Maria remembered. "Cinthya was one and a half years old. She thought the snow was a sandy beach. She took off her shoes and socks and stood there in shock! It was warm in the apartment. [She wondered] why was this 'white sand' so cold?"

Living in Los Angeles and Chicago had been difficult. For Maria, living in Madison was even worse. Maria said, "People would smile . . . but nobody spoke Spanish. I was totally, totally **isolated** [**i** suh **la** ted, separated from everyone else]. I cried every night. I wanted to go home."

Maria was lonely, afraid, and pregnant again. She decided to move closer to her mother, who now lived in Chicago. There Maria worked as a dishwasher for $1.25 an hour. Her mother helped with the children. "Ismael worked everywhere. Making tortillas. House painting. At one point he had four jobs. Four!" Maria remembered.

Making Tamales

This is a scene from my parents' kitchen. Everybody is making tamales. My grandfather is wearing blue overalls and a blue shirt. I'm right next to him with my sister Margie. We're helping to soak the dried leaves from the corn. My mother is spreading the cornmeal dough on the leaves and my aunt and uncle are spreading meat on the dough. My grandmother is lining up the rolled and folded tamales ready for cooking. In some families just the women make tamales, but in our family everybody helps.

La Tamalada

Ésta es una escena de la cocina de mis padres. Todos están haciendo tamales. Mi abuelo tiene puesto rancheros azules y camisa azul. Yo estoy al lado de él, con mi hermana Margie. Estamos ayudando a remojar las hojas secas del maíz. Mi Mamá está esparciendo la masa de maíz sobre las hojas, y mis tíos están esparciendo la carne sobre la masa. Mi abuelita está ordenando los tamales que ya están enrollados, cubiertos y listos para cocer. En algunas familias sólo las mujeres preparan tamales, pero en mi familia todos ayudan.

These pages are from Family Pictures/Cuadros de Familia, *a book written in both Spanish and English. How would you feel if you had to move to a country and go to school without being able to speak the language of everyone around you?*

The years in Chicago were really hard. Ismael's father died, and Ismael returned to Mexico for almost six months. Another baby was born. Gang violence exploded in their neighborhood. Drugs were sold in front of Cinthya's school. Maria had just started to learn English at the library when gang members robbed Ismael and Maria and threatened to burn down their house. Afraid for their children, they returned to Madison.

There the same loneliness returned, hanging over Maria like a dark storm cloud. Finally, when her baby got sick and she didn't know how to call a doctor, she decided that somehow she had to learn English. "Cinthya was in kindergarten. The ESL [English as a Second Language] teacher in her school told me about MATC [Madison Area Technical College]. I knew I had to go." Maria said that she and the four children "would sit in the back of the room for one and a half hours, but I had to learn English. I had to know how to speak for myself. To stop crying and do something about it."

The long bus rides were worth it. Maria learned English. One by one, the children started kindergarten. Maria began to work as a teacher's aide in the Madison Public Schools. Maria's dreams didn't end with one English class. She continued at MATC. She got a **scholarship** (**skah** lur ship, money for school) that opened the door for her to study education at the University of Wisconsin at Madison and become a schoolteacher. Studying helped turn Maria's dreams into reality. But making those dreams come true was harder than anyone imagined. Telling the story makes Maria cry and laugh all at once.

Ismael worked hard, and the children helped, which made Maria very proud of them. "We all took care of each other," she remembers. "I never would have believed . . . not in a million years that I would [be able to] . . . go to the university. My professor encouraged me so much. I started to believe that *yes*, I could do it. . . . All of us together, we did it.

This is the Covarrubias family in 2001. From left to right, Daniel, Maria, Cinthya, Hector, Jorge, Julia, and Ismael.

On May 28, 1998, Wisconsin celebrated its 150th birthday as a state. Maria and Ismael Covarrubias had a very special celebration that day, too. They became U.S. citizens. In 1986, a new immigration law granted **amnesty** (**am** nis tee, official forgiveness) to some immigrants who had entered the country illegally. Maria and Ismael wrote to U.S.

71

President Ronald Reagan in 1986. They explained why they had crossed the border illegally, and Maria said, "We apologized." The U.S. government granted them amnesty, but it took many more years before they could become citizens. To become citizens, they had to live in the same house in the same community for five years.

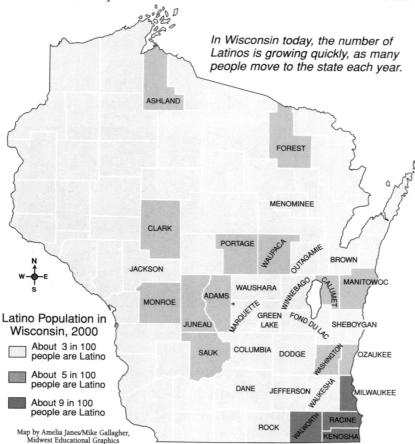

In Wisconsin today, the number of Latinos is growing quickly, as many people move to the state each year.

Latino Population in Wisconsin, 2000

About 3 in 100 people are Latino

About 5 in 100 people are Latino

About 9 in 100 people are Latino

Map by Amelia Janes/Mike Gallagher, Midwest Educational Graphics

They had to study and pass a test. They did it! On Statehood Day, 1998, Maria and Ismael were sworn in as U.S. citizens. At noon, bells rang in honor of Wisconsin's birthday. Maria said, "We could hear bells ringing all over Madison." As the Covarrubias family celebrated, Wisconsin was celebrating as well.

Today Maria and Ismael Covarrubias live in Madison. Cinthya is studying to become a lawyer. Jorge, Daniel, Hector, and Julie are all students in high school or college. Maria is a teacher at Chavez Elementary School.

Looking Back, Looking Forward

You've met real people who made the journey to Wisconsin across oceans aboard ships or planes. Some traveled from other parts of the United States by train or wagon—or on foot.

But all who came here left behind families and friends and familiar places they loved. And all brought things they thought they would need on their journeys and things they hoped would help them when they arrived. They tried to anticipate difficulties, but many met dangers that surprised them and problems that they had to overcome. Their adventures became part of their family stories—stories they told to their children, wrote about in diaries, journals, letters, or **memoirs** (**mem** wars, stories remembered and written years later). Everyone dreams and wishes for a bright future. Would those dreams be enough to help them settle in a new home in Wisconsin?

Unit 3
Settling in Wisconsin

◆ ◆ ◆

Chances are you've heard your teacher ask students to *settle down* after recess or lunch. Settling down is hard. Settling into a new classroom at the beginning of a school year is difficult, too. It takes a while to feel like you actually belong. In the same way, the experience of settling in Wisconsin was hard for newcomers, whether they arrived a hundred years ago or just last month.

Once people reached Wisconsin, they often found that the hard times weren't over. For many families, that first year of

These are the kinds of stories you'll read about in this unit.

 **Searching for Home**

 Working to Live

 Weathering Wisconsin

 Making a Home

 Homesick

TIMELINE

These are the people you will meet in this unit, and these are the dates when they first settled in Wisconsin.

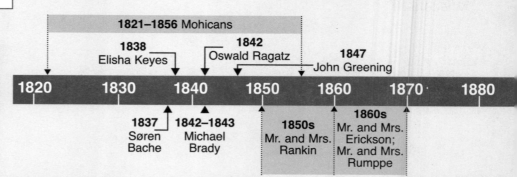

1821–1856 Mohicans

1838 Elisha Keyes

1842 Oswald Ragatz

1847 John Greening

| 1820 | 1830 | 1840 | 1850 | 1860 | 1870 | 1880 |

1837 Søren Bache

1842–1843 Michael Brady

1850s Mr. and Mrs. Rankin

1860s Mr. and Mrs. Erickson; Mr. and Mrs. Rumppe

74

settling down felt more like a struggle just to survive. Life was work and more work. The first challenge was finding a place to live. That meant looking for a farm or an apartment in the city. Farmers had to clear land. City-dwellers had to find jobs. Winter was especially hard. As time passed, loneliness and homesickness crept in, making life harder still.

Coming to Wisconsin was only the beginning. Newcomers had to "settle in." They did this by working, saving, and planning day by day and month by month, to make a home for themselves. These new arrivals worried. Where will we live? Where will we work? How will we handle Wisconsin's cold winters? How will we deal with homesickness for people and places left behind? Those worries made the first year in Wisconsin especially hard for everyone. In this unit, you'll read stories of the struggle to settle down. But you will also learn about the strength and hope that helped people claim Wisconsin as their new home.

1892
Kanter Family

1976–2001
Mayhoua Moua

1890   1900   1910   1920   1970   1980   1990   2000

1917–1918
Rubie Bond;
Blue Jenkins

Searching for Home

We have followed Oswald Ragatz, the Nattestad brothers, the Kanter family, and others who wrote or told about their journeys to Wisconsin. Each of their stories tells us about *one* person or *one* family who chose or was forced to leave an old home and find a new one.

But the Mohicans were an entire *community* of people looking for a permanent place to make a home. Their move to Wisconsin was very different from the journeys of the other people described in this book.

Great Waters That Are Never Still

The Mohicans are *Native* people. Since long ago, the name they call themselves is "Muh-he-con-nuk," meaning "Great Waters That Are Never Still." The official name of those who live in Wisconsin is Mohican Nation Stockbridge-Munsee Band, and this long name is another part of their story. The Mohicans have passed down stories from the time of their **ancestors** (an **ses** turs, relatives who lived long ago).

Like the Oneida tribe, the Mohican tribe had a home here in North America long before Europeans ever tried to sail across the Atlantic Ocean. But once Europeans arrived, the Mohican people moved again and again. They moved from New York to Massachusetts, then back to New York. Then they moved from New York to Indiana, and on to Wisconsin. And in Wisconsin, the Mohican tribe *still* had to move. But the community they have made here has helped them survive as a people. This is the story of their many journeys. You can follow the routes on the map.

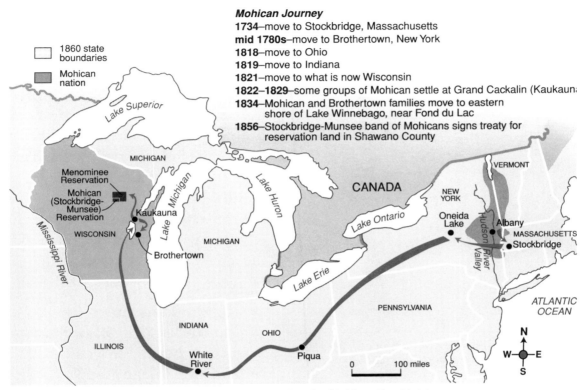

Mohican Journey
1734–move to Stockbridge, Massachusetts
mid 1780s–move to Brothertown, New York
1818–move to Ohio
1819–move to Indiana
1821–move to what is now Wisconsin
1822–1829–some groups of Mohican settle at Grand Cackalin (Kaukaun;
1834–Mohican and Brothertown families move to eastern
  shore of Lake Winnebago, near Fond du Lac
1856–Stockbridge-Munsee band of Mohicans signs treaty for
  reservation land in Shawano County

This map shows the long journey over many years that the Mohican Stockbridge-Munsee Band made to Wisconsin. Map by Amelia Janes/Mike Gallagher, Midwest Educational Graphics

The Mohicans tell of life long ago in New York's Hudson River Valley, where they hunted and planted gardens that included squash, corn, beans, and sunflowers. They traded with (and sometimes fought against) other Native people. There were good times and bad times before the first Europeans came in the 1700s. Then the Mohican way of life changed forever.

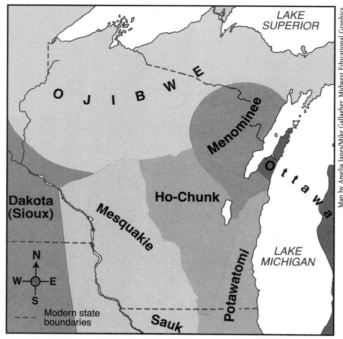

LAKE SUPERIOR

OJIBWE

Menominee

Ottawa

Dakota (Sioux)

Mesquakie

Ho-Chunk

LAKE MICHIGAN

Potawatomi

Sauk

N
W—E
S

Modern state boundaries

Map by Amelia Janes/Mike Gallagher, Midwest Educational Graphics

This map shows the general areas where different tribal people lived in Wisconsin before Europeans arrived.

Trading furs with Europeans caused disagreements between the Mohicans and their Mohawk neighbors. When the Mohicans fought against the Mohawks, many lives were lost. Even more Mohican people got sick from diseases the Europeans brought with them. They were a much smaller and weaker group when they met European **missionaries** (**mish** shun air reez), religious people who told them about the Christian idea of God. Many Mohican people became Christians.

The Mohicans moved from New York to Stockbridge, Massachusetts, where they hoped life would be better. Other Indian groups that had become Christians joined them in Stockbridge. In 1734, European neighbors began to call the Mohican people (and all the other Indians in the community) "Stockbridge Indians" after the name of their town. The Mohican families went to church and sent their children to community schools with non-Indian children. They learned to read and write. They learned new skills from their European neighbors. Some Mohican adults became teachers. Others became shopkeepers. Perhaps they no longer practiced some of their ceremonies.

More Europeans arrived. New white settlers pushed the Mohicans from their homes. Life in Stockbridge was no longer the same.

In the mid-1780s, the Mohican Stockbridge people moved on again. This time they were granted land by the Oneida in what is now Madison County, New York. Land companies wanted to sell land to white settlers. These land companies wanted—and got—Indian land. Indian land was supposed to be protected by **treaty** (an official agreement between governments) between tribal people and the U.S. government. But the government did not honor this treaty. And once again, the Mohicans were on the move.

In 1818, two groups of Mohican people left New York. One group traveled west to join the Munsee tribe in Indiana. It was a long way to travel.

Tribal member Sheila Powless remembers her family's stories about this journey. "I remember my Uncle Bert telling how his mother walked

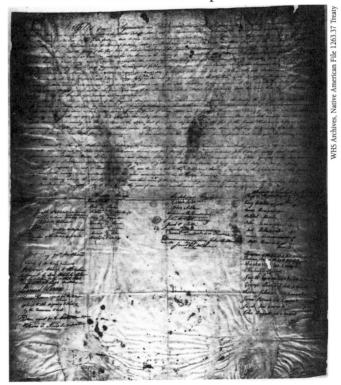

This treaty was signed by Oneida, Stockbridge, and St. Regis chiefs on January 8, 1825.

from New York to Indiana. He grew up hearing the story. [His mother] was only five years old. And they walked, probably beside wagons or ox carts."

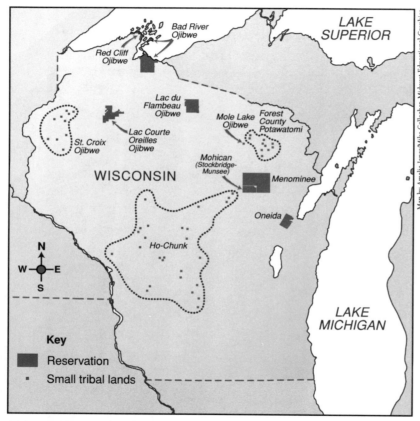

This map shows tribal lands of the Native people in Wisconsin today. You can see that the Mohican and Stockbridge-Munsee reservation lands are in the southwest corner of an area that once was Menominee land.

The group spent the first winter in Ohio. By the time the Mohicans reached Indiana, they found that the Delaware had been forced to move farther west. Where would the Mohicans of Stockbridge go? In 1821, they traveled all the way to present-day Wisconsin, then part of Michigan Territory.

But their journey to find a permanent home was not over. Again the groups divided. Some Mohicans settled at Grand Cackalin (known today as Kaukauna in east-central Wisconsin). But white settlers wanted land near the Fox River, too.

In 1834, Mohican families moved to the eastern shore of Lake Winnebago, not far from Fond du Lac. Other Mohicans moving from New York joined them there. Again they had trouble with land-greedy settlers. Some Mohicans and a group of Munsee moved farther west. Some stayed behind. "You see, our people were always moving," Sheila Powless explained. "They always had to move. When I was small I would lie on the floor and ask, 'Where did people live? What happened then?' Uncle Bert would tell me and I would draw roads and maps, showing where our people were."

Finally, in 1856, Mohican Elder John W. Quinney helped make a new treaty. This was to be the last treaty. It granted the Stockbridge-Munsee Band of the Mohicans land in Shawano County that had once belonged to the Menominee tribe.

The moving ended, but the remembering will always go on. "This is a hard story," said Mohican Elder Dorothy Davids. "But we've survived. We've *survived*. We've lived longer right here in Wisconsin than anywhere since European arrival. We've survived. . . . And we are Indians. . . . Always, always Indians."

Elder John W. Quinney was the Mohican leader who helped his people find a permanent home on tribal land in Shawano County.

Working to Live

Whether newcomers came from Europe or from other places in the United States, they all faced hard work. Those journal-keepers and letter-writers who had scribbled page after page while crossing the ocean were suddenly too overworked and exhausted to write a word. Remember Michael Brady, who had sailed from Ireland in 1842? While at sea he filled his journal with stories. Then he arrived in New York, found work, and was too busy to write in that journal for almost a year! Between January and November of 1843 he managed to enter only three sentences in his journal: "March the 1st hired 8 months with Mr. Barns. Worked very hard, bought no clothes. Received payment."

Work and More Work

Think back to Oswald Ragatz's family. In 1842, they spent nine weeks on the ocean, almost two weeks traveling on the Mississippi River, and another week crossing Wisconsin in a wagon. The family arrived in Sauk City tired, sick, and wondering if they made the right choice to leave Switzerland. Still, the Ragatz family had to find land and clear it. With a horse, a plow, sweat, and muscle, they had to turn

82

Illustration by Jill Bremigan

prairie grass and Wisconsin forest into farmland. They had to build some kind of shelter—*anything*—to keep out the cold. Somehow they had to store enough food for the long winter.

You also read about John Greening, who wrote about his 1847 journey to the United States aboard the *Radius*. Once settled in Black Earth, he wrote about the work immigrants had to do. "When they come to a prairie they shoot for meat, roast corn for coffee . . . and sleep in their wagons at night. . . . [Prairie] sod here is so tough that it takes 6 yoke of oxen to break it up." A plowman and ox team could be hired for $2 per acre in Mazomanie, but John didn't have that much money. He used what he did have to rent four oxen and then did the plowing himself.

Working Women

When you read about hard work, do you imagine *men* chopping firewood, wrestling with a horse-drawn plow, or driving a wagon? Women worked just as hard—sometimes harder.

Before the first winter came, a new settler had to clear a small plot of land and build a house to give the family shelter.

There's an old saying that a woman's work is never done. Women cared for children and did all the household work without washers, dryers, dishwashers, or other things that make housekeeping easier today.

83

Everyone in the family was needed to run a farm, as you can see from this picture of a young boy working a plow drawn by four huge horses.

WHS Archives, CF 53119

Most women worked caring for their families. It was a mother's job to cook and clean. She made soap and stitched the family's clothes by hand. She grew vegetables in the garden, milked the cow, and made cheese and butter. If the school was far away, she might teach her children, too. At night, when even a hard-working father could finally snatch a moment's rest, a mother's knitting needles were still clicking.

Oswald Ragatz saw how hard his mother worked. Years later, he remembered, "I think mother [felt] the heaviest burden of our move to America." His father and the boys worked twelve or even more hours a day plowing, planting, hunting, or harvesting. But his mother's work seemed endless. Oswald wrote, "She never complained, though . . . her day was always longest."

Nine Dollars a Week and All the Meat We Can Eat

Azriel Kanter and his family had escaped the pogroms of Russia. When they arrived in New York, Azriel worked hard as a butcher, but he could barely feed his family. So Rosa and the children went to live with friends in Chicago, and they saved what they could. Azriel had to move from job to job, always working to save enough money to join his family.

Azriel received a letter from a relative with news of a butchering job in Green Bay. Azriel wanted a steady job, but he felt uneasy. *Wisconsin?* He'd never even heard of such a place. He imagined a wilderness filled with wolves and wild animals. He described his worries in his journal, "Why should I be able to earn my bit of bread in some other way . . . to be stuck in a small place, barely—just barely—managing to scratch out a **livelihood** [money for living] and with no hope of getting out. But, good or bad, I can no longer remain here."

Azriel was desperate. He took the job in Green Bay because it paid nine dollars a week and all the meat he and his family could eat! And most importantly, he and his wife and children could live together again.

Doing the Dirty Work

Think of Rubie Bond. Her father didn't have to build a log cabin, but his work was still very, very hard. The Fairbanks-Morse Company in Beloit offered jobs to African American men like Rubie's papa, jobs that no white workers wanted to do. African American men worked in the **foundry,** where metal was melted and shaped. This work was dirty, dangerous, and backbreaking. The work shifts were long. But Rubie's papa and the other men took those jobs anyway. As sharecroppers, they could never save money. At least the foundry jobs offered a chance to get ahead.

WHS Archives, CF 629

This photograph shows a Milwaukee foundry in 1951. Foundries in cities like Beloit, Racine, and Milwaukee needed workers who would take jobs that no one else wanted. Many African Americans, including Rubie Bond's father, came to Wisconsin to work at jobs like this.

85

Weathering Wisconsin

Wisconsin is a four-season state where the weather is always changing. Our winters can be snowy and freezing. Our summers can be hot and sticky. Wisconsin weather was a real problem for new settlers long ago.

People look forward to the warmth of summer, but they don't look forward to the mosquitoes! Wet summers bring mosquitoes by the millions. For those in frontier Wisconsin, **malaria** (muh **lair** ee uh, sickness spread by mosquitoes) was a constant worry. Armies of malaria-carrying mosquitoes made life miserable. Homesteaders kept smoky fires going twenty-four hours a day to keep the pests away. Still, the poor animals suffered, and the children were bitten until they cried.

Summer meant heat and mosquitoes. Winter brought danger and even death.

A String of Lights in the Cold

On a late winter afternoon in the mid-1800s, a boat filled with Scottish immigrants landed in at the harbor in Ephraim (**e** frum) in Door County. There wasn't a cabin or shelter in sight. As the sun set and a bitter wind blew across the shore, the immigrants huddled

This blizzard took place in Whitewater in March 1881. Snow was very hard on new arrivals from warmer climates.

WHS Archives, CF 1773

together. They knew that only a miracle would save them from freezing to death. Years later, the grandson of one of those Scotsmen told the story:

"The boat crashed into the rocks and ice and the Scots came ashore cold and wet . . . freezing and with little hope of surviving the night. There was no town in sight, but as nightfall came, they saw a moving light. Then, a whole string of lights like torches, coming over the hill. It was a group of Norwegian skiers! . . . They took them home and shared what they had until spring. . . . The Norwegians too were newcomers in a strange land, and they welcomed the opportunity to learn English [from their new Scottish friends.] It was said [later] that they were the only group of Norwegians in the state who spoke English with a Scottish accent!"

Sparks Lead to Fire

Weather could be a farmer's best friend or worst enemy. Would the rain come? Would the sun shine? If the summer was dry and hot, a spark could start a prairie fire that would devour whole towns, leaving behind nothing but ashes.

In the hills between Mazomanie and Black Earth, John Greening from England saw one fire that lasted a week.

The Peshtigo fire in 1872 was the worst fire in Wisconsin history, destroying land and towns and killing thousands of people.

"Last night we had fires blazing, rushing and crashing in all directions," he wrote. "This morning all was burned as black as a cinder for 50 miles. The fires run through the country as fast as a horse can trot, and sometimes faster. . . . I have been across the wide marsh to the banks of the Wisconsin river. . . . Trees 50 feet long . . . burnt and falling in all directions with a crash that makes the earth tremble."

The First Winter

In Wisconsin, winter often starts before Christmas and hangs on until April—sometimes longer. If settlers found the work backbreaking, they found the first winter heartbreaking. The days were cold, and the nights were colder. Sometimes ice formed on the walls *inside* houses. Food froze in the cupboards, and snow piled up so high that it reached second-story windows. And then the blizzards came, hitting without warning. Wind whipped the snow into a blinding whirl. An inexperienced newcomer might go out to do chores and get lost between the house and the barn. He'd be found, frozen solid, when the blizzard passed.

WHS Archives, CF 5488

People needed huge amounts of firewood to keep the house warm during a long, cold Wisconsin winter like this one in Marinette County in 1955.

Søren Bache came to Muskego from Norway in 1837. Even icy Norwegian winters hadn't prepared him for January in Wisconsin. Søren wrote, "When temperatures were lowest, people could not do much work. . . . The stove was always kept red-hot. Anyone seated near the stove ran the risk of being burned on one side while freezing on the other. Ice sometimes formed on fresh milk before we could get it from the barn to the house . . . we almost **perished** [**pair** ishd, died] from cold, indoors and out."

During the Ragatzes' first Wisconsin winter, Oswald's father was in Sauk City when a blizzard hit. He had never seen such a storm in his life and was wild with worry for his wife and children. He fought his way home through drifts and blinding snow. When Mr. Ragatz reached home, he stumbled into the house, half-frozen. For weeks he lay sick, feverish, and coughing blood. For the rest of his life, his lungs were weak because of frostbite.

Family and friends back in Europe were horrified at the stories. "The cold has dropped to 28 below freezing," John Greening wrote his family in England after moving to Black Earth in 1847. "Water freezes within a yard of the fire. If you spit, 'tis ice before it reaches the ground."

Winter's End

Spring! Wouldn't you just count the days until winter passed? Just think, no more blindly following a guide rope from the house to the barn in the middle of a blizzard. No more stuffing rags beneath the door to keep out the cold. No more begging the landlord for more coal. For many newcomers, the first spring brought more than warm weather, it brought hope.

At the first sign of spring, Søren Bache was wild with joy. He wrote, "At last! No longer would we need to hug the stove, burning our **trousers** [**trow** zurs, pants] [or] hibernate like bears. . . . Thank heavens, we could now escape like birds from their cages."

A Fish Story

Other folks, like Elisha Keyes and his family, were glad to see spring because they were just plain hungry. In 1838, the Keyes family had moved from the eastern United States to Lake Mills. They were city folks, totally unprepared for pioneer life, especially in Wisconsin. The men were such bad hunters that they scared away the deer. They tried to catch fish with the wrong bait. Come spring, their flour sacks were empty, the potatoes were long gone, and their stomachs were growling.

Snow still clung to the hollows along the creek when Elisha and his brother were sent to water the horses. Suddenly, Elisha began to shout with excitement. *Fish!* The stream was filled with suckerfish as long as Elisha's arm. The boys raced home, hollering to anyone they could find. They'd have fish for supper tonight!

So many fish! Elisha, his family, and their neighbors would be able to eat all the fish they could catch.

Illustration by Sue Manske

Everyone rushed to the stream armed with pitchforks, shovels, pokers, or anything they could use to scoop, pull, trap, or spear a fish. Elisha's father grabbed a wheelbarrow. A neighbor brought a wagon.

Those fish saved their lives. "We had fish for breakfast, fish for dinner, and fish for supper, and fish all the time," Elisha said. The whole neighborhood joked that they ate nothing but fish until the bones stuck right through their skin so they couldn't take off their shirts for months!

Making a Home

Weather was not the only problem for newcomers. During that hard first year, they had to build, rent, or buy their shelter. For settlers in the country, building a log cabin took weeks. Lucky families had neighbors to help. Unlucky folks worked alone, cutting and hauling trees and then rolling and lifting the logs, one at a time, until four walls were built. In cities, finding shelter meant renting an apartment that the family could afford and hoping that the neighborhood would not be too dangerous. Only those who had plenty of money could buy a house immediately.

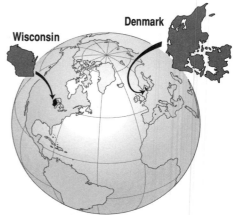

Map by Amelia Janes/Mike Gallagher, Midwest Educational Graphics

One Fork to Share

In Shennington, a town in western Wisconsin, an immigrant woman from Denmark wrote about life in that first difficult year of 1881. "Ten dollars was all we had besides the clothes we wore and a few old ones in our trunk. My husband had to go to work at once in the cranberry marsh [for] . . . a dollar and a half a day. . . . I picked berries at seventy-five cents a bushel.

Everything the Danish family in Shennington had for cooking and eating could be placed on one table.

For an extra quilt we used a fur coat that we had taken along from Denmark. An old cook stove . . . left by some lumbermen, we found in the woods and fixed. . . . Three plates, two cups and saucers, two knives, one fork, a frying pan, and a kettle completed the outfit of our new home."

New Home, School, and Neighborhood

Of course, Rubie Bond's family didn't ride across the prairie in a wheat wagon, they took the train from Pontotoc, Mississippi, to Beloit. Rubie remembered being on the train when it chugged into Beloit station.

Rubie said, "My first impression of Beloit? Well, it was 1,000 miles north and I was just ten. My grandfather went to find a place to live. Then, snow! Snow! It was so cold. And I went to school. Not a Mississippi school, but a good school with art and music. . . . [In Mississippi we had] eight grades in two rooms . . . with a leaky roof. And the white children went to school in a brick building."

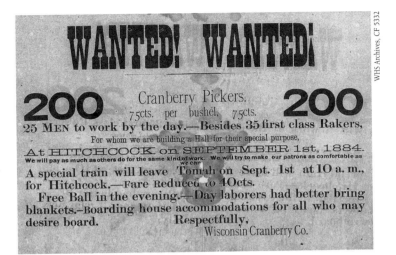

WHS Archives, CF 5332

WANTED! WANTED!

200 Cranberry Pickers. **200**
75cts. per bushel, 75cts.
25 MEN to work by the day.—Besides 35 first class Rakers,
For whom we are building a Hall for their special purpose,
At HITCHCOCK on SEPTEMBER 1st, 1884.
We will pay as much as others do for the same kind of work. We will try to make our patrons as comfortable as we can.
A special train will leave Tomah on Sept. 1st at 10 a. m., for Hitchcock.—Fare Reduced to 40cts.
Free Ball in the evening.—Day laborers had better bring blankets.—Boarding house accommodations for all who may desire board.　　Respectfully,
Wisconsin Cranberry Co.

At harvest time, getting the crops picked takes lots of workers. In this 1884 poster, how much was the farmer offering to pay?

93

Like the Bonds, the Harrell family left sharecropping behind in Pontotoc, Mississippi, to work for Fairbanks Morse in Beloit. They lived in Fairbanks Flats. From left to right, the children are Buford, Emma, George, and Jesse (on George's lap). This photograph was taken in 1942.

Rubie's father didn't have to cut trees to build a log cabin, but the family still had to find work and a place to live. For African Americans, housing was a problem. White landlords often refused to rent to black families. The Fairbanks Morse Company built special apartment buildings for the black workers and their families. These apartment buildings were so boxy and flat that people called them Fairbanks Flats.

"Send Them All Back"

Black workers also came to Beloit from the Caribbean islands of Cuba, Jamaica, and Barbados. These men found work in Wisconsin, but their families lived thousands of miles away. They were

This is the way Fairbanks Flats looked in 1981. It's easy to see how they got their nickname.

paid less than white workers. Sometimes they were even paid less than African American workers from the American South like Rubie's papa.

Many landlords wouldn't rent to the workers from Cuba, Jamaica, and Barbados. These newcomers had to live in crowded "camps" owned by the factories where they worked. They slept on cots and ate on tin plates. Blue Jenkins, an African American elder from Racine, remembered those years:

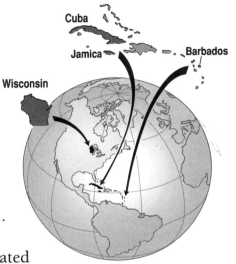

Map by Amelia Janes/Mike Gallagher, Midwest Educational Graphics

"They **recruited** [re **cru** ted, hired] a lot of blacks . . . brought these guys over here [from the islands] and . . . they misused these guys. . . . They were really discriminated against. . . . Then, when the war was over, what really **put icing on the cake** [made things even worse] was the whites wanted those jobs . . . you know, wanted the blacks out. . . . They knew they couldn't make the Southerners go back South, but they could get the Jamaicans and Barbadians out of there . . . and one of the guys got up in the **union** [organization of workers] meeting and said, 'Send [them all] back in cattle cars if we have to.' "

By 1918, World War II had ended. White workers returning from the army took the jobs, and the Caribbean workers were sent back to Cuba, Jamaica, and Barbados. For them, Wisconsin was not a place of hope, but a place of discrimination and disappointment.

Homesick

Most of us have been the new person somewhere: new to a classroom, new to a neighborhood, new to a scout troop or ball team. When you're new, nothing feels quite comfortable. You sometimes feel alone. And that's when you miss the things and the people and places that make you feel "at home." Everyone who ever moved to Wisconsin felt those same feelings, especially at the beginning.

Frontier Loneliness

It was the loneliness that made that first hard year even harder. One autumn in the 1850s, a Finnish farmer named Mr. Rankin found work as a lumberjack. Taking the job meant he'd be gone all winter, but he couldn't turn down paying work. He knew his wife would be safe in their cozy cabin in the western area of the state, near Sparta, so Mr. Rankin pulled on his woolen **longjohns** (long underwear), grabbed his axe, hugged his wife one last time, and set off for the lumber camps.

Map by Amelia Janes/Mike Gallagher,
Midwest Educational Graphics

That whole winter Mrs. Rankin was absolutely alone, without a single neighbor. She fed the animals alone. She baked bread and did the washing alone. In the evenings she sat knitting—still alone. Month after month she worked and waited. October passed. Then November. As slow as turtles, December, January, February, and March crawled by. Finally, one April day, spring returned, and finally Mr. Rankin came home. Mrs. Rankin must have been very happy to see, hear, and talk to another person again, especially her husband.

Even long days of work couldn't help Oswald Ragatz's mother forget her loneliness. During the family's first spring in Wisconsin, she cried and cried. She wondered if they had made a terrible mistake coming to America. In Switzerland they had not been rich, but at least the children went to school. Now that they lived in Sauk City, the nearest school was miles away. The children worked instead of learning to read. They hauled stones from the fields instead of going to school. What's more, there was no church except a traveling preacher who showed up every few months.

Men like Mr. Rankin worked as lumberjacks in winter. It was easier to haul logs by sled over snow and ice.

Why had they left Switzerland? Wisconsin seemed wild and empty in comparison. "Why, it will be a thousand years before this land is settled up," Oswald's mother worried. "Our children and all who follow them for generations to come will be **uncouth peasants**" (un **kooth pez** entz, poor people without manners or education).

Even if Oswald Ragatz's family had lived near a school, it would probably have had only one room—for kids of all ages. This classroom was in a log schoolhouse built in Weston in 1897.

Clothes for a Cow

Norwegian immigrants Olaf and Ingeborg (**ing** a borg) Erickson moved to a tiny community near Cashton in western Wisconsin in the 1860s. They passed down the

following story about their neighbor, Mrs. Rumppe. Mrs. Rumppe was a sixteen-year-old bride from Germany when she and her husband bought their land. That first year was hard. Mr. Rumppe **hired out to work** (worked for someone else) while Mrs. Rumppe "stayed alone in their log cabin all week. The only other living being on the place, beside the wild animals, was their cow. One weekend she decided to wash and iron her one and only skirt. There was no clothes line, so the skirt was hung to dry on the rail fence." Mrs. Rumppe went to borrow a bit of flour from the neighbors, and, "when she returned, the cow had chewed up her skirt! She cried all evening, for there was no money to buy material for another." Mrs. Rumppe had to wear her petticoats with no skirt all summer!

The Ericksons' log cabin near Cashton probably looked very much like this one, built in 1865 by Nels Spillman near Hartland. His wife and four children are outside. Like the Ericksons, the Spillmans didn't have neighbors close by.

What a year! The bride and her new husband had no friends, no money, and almost no food. "When they started haying, there was little food left except potatoes. . . . Their cow was **fresh** [producing milk], so they had milk. They had just enough flour left. . . . They had potatoes and gravy for breakfast, dinner, and supper for three straight weeks."

Of course, newcomers were homesick. Many immigrants lived near others from their homelands. Just hearing the familiar language of home or eating traditional foods eased the pain and sadness. Other

Illustration by Susan Manske

Mrs. Rumppe was really shocked to find the cow eating her only skirt!

people like the Mohican Indians or Hmong refugees came to Wisconsin in groups and tried hard to stay together.

For most people, homesickness was a sadness that came and passed. But others were not so lucky. For someone living in a cabin miles from the nearest neighbor, homesickness could be dangerous. It could linger on and on, until sadness became **depression** (de **preh** shun; deep, long-lasting sadness). The nights were long. Days were filled with work, work, work. Neighbors were few and often far away. Farm work left little time for visiting. Women often had to remain home alone with babies and hard chores.

Even after the fields were clear and crops planted, farm work was always demanding.

WHS Archives, CF 537

Remembering Home

Sometimes small memories of home brought big waves of homesickness. Immigrants missed the taste of real German sausage or rich, brown Norwegian goat cheese. At unexpected moments, memories of sugar-topped Christmas cakes or lighting **Sabbath** (Jewish weekly day of rest) candles on a Friday evening could bring tears to a settler's eyes. "I would give anything to hear a German lark sing," one immigrant wrote. "I close my eyes and see my mother's face," wrote another.

In time, new experiences in America took away some of the homesickness. John Greening missed the singing of English birds until he found another sweet sound to take its place. "We have no singing birds here," he wrote, "but their loss is made up by crickets and grasshoppers that we hear sing and creak for half a mile. Just before rain they make a wonderful noise."

Spring also softened the sting of homesickness. When the first purple and yellow crocuses peeked through the melting snow, those heavy, homesick feelings began to fade. In their place, hope sprouted.

Photo by Donna Krischan

When flowers like this bloomed in early spring, hope began to replace homesickness.

A Closer Look

Always Hmong

Whether newcomers come to Wisconsin from across the ocean or across the state border, they carry with them memories and the culture of their homelands. How will they hold on to memories and traditions while making a new home here? What will be lost? These are worries for everyone. And every family finds its own answer. This is the story of Mayhoua Moua (my **ooh** ah **moo** ah). This is how she and her family found their answer.

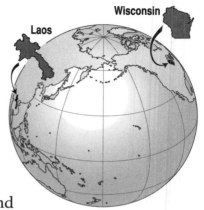

Map by Amelia Janes/Mike Gallagher, Midwest Educational Graphics

Mayhoua Moua was born in Laos in 1969. Her people, the Hmong (mung), lived peaceful lives in the highlands of Thailand (**ty** land), Laos (**lah** os), and Vietnam (**vee** et **nahm**). When the United States entered the Vietnam War in the 1960s, the Hmong way of life changed forever. The Hmong people fought on the American side.

Courtesy of Mayhoua Moua

This photograph of Mayhoua's family was taken in the refugee camp in Thailand in 1975. From left to right in the back row are her mother, Blia Yang, her youngest brother, Touyang Ly, and her father, Chong Ly. In the front row are her two sisters, Mayechy and Maychoua. Mayhoua is standing next to her dad.

102

Mayhoua's father was a soldier when the United States lost the war, and Mayhoua's family was in danger in Laos. They ran for their lives to Thailand. Mayhoua still remembers.

"We prepared to cross the Mekong River. It was late at night. My Uncle's house was full of people waiting to get smuggled out. . . . Before dawn my mother woke us. All the women and children were put in taxis . . . and the elders, too. We were so afraid. The children cried. We pushed the cars to be silent. Pushed until daylight."

Mayhoua Moua lived in three different **refugee camps** (safe, but not permanent, places for refugees) in Thailand in one year! Her father worked very hard to get his family to America. At last, a church agreed to **sponsor** (officially help) them. The family would fly to America from Hong Kong.

Mayhoua said, "I remember the airport in Hong Kong. My brother was just a baby.

It was always hard when some family members left and others stayed behind. This photo was taken around 1985 at Ban Vinai Refugee Camp in Thailand.

During the war, Hmong families had to move often, searching for a safe place to stay.

Watertown Public Opinion, August 27, 1976

WATERTOWN PUBLIC OPINION

VOLUME 88   Price 15c   Associated Press   NUMBER 204

WATERTOWN, S.D., FRIDAY, AUGUST 27, 1976

Laotian family here

The Ly family has arrived. That is, they are at home in Webster after fleeing their homeland in Laos following the communist take-over, which made Laos an unsafe place for Buddhists who had been employed by the United States Army.

So far, local committees indicate there are numerous minor problems but none as big as the ones which forced them to break off all contact with their family background, traditions and customs and throw themselves on the mercy of friends half a world away.

The family includes Chong Ly (say it 'Lee'), 30, who has been a clerk for the U.S. Army in Laos; Blia Yang Chong, 28, who has an extremely limited English vocabulary plus French vocabulary...

bridge from Laotian to English by taking advantage of Mrs. Ly's French. Mrs. DeJong is qualified to teach French. Still another aid to communications has appeared with the arrival of Mrs. Bradford Pigors of Ferney, herself a Laotian, who can help the Lys to become Americans.

Anxious to find employment

Mrs. Ly has a brother, who now lives in France, and who has written a history of his homeland. She has a primary school education but no commercial skills, being a housewife. Mr. Ly has more than normal education for a Laotian and has achieved the rating of Warrant Officer with the U.S. Army while employed by them in Laos between 1961 and 1972. He has indicated he is anxious to find some sort of employment here and again become self sufficient as the family's breadwinner.

Meanwhile, the Lys are making their home in an apartment here which was furnished through efforts of the sponsoring church committees from St. John's Lutheran, American Lutheran

and United Methodist. About all they lack at the moment, sponsors say, is the same as the rest of us, cash. "Laotian Family" funds have been established at both Webster banks to assist in providing needed money for food and basic necessities for the time being.

They arrived in Watertown by commercial airline Thursday evening and were greeted by 22 persons from Webster. The group then drove to Webster where the Lys were taken to their apartment and welcomed by additional people who hosted a coffee and cookie lunch.

The Lys are among a few families being assisted in escaping from the refugee camp in Thailand after fleeing their homeland following the communist take-over in the Far East. For one who was a Buddhist and who had been friendly with the Americans, he was unpopular, to say the least, with the new ruling powers. Officials said the Lys would have had no future at home under current conditions there.

(Continued on Page 16)

I remember dragging our stuff. Hmong and Lao people were everywhere. I was nearly 7 years old. We got on this huge airplane. HUGE . . . so it seemed to me then. An American boy gave us pins . . . airline wings. . . . He talked and talked and talked, and I couldn't understand a word!"

Mayhoua's family had always lived in a village tucked among the green hills of Laos. Their first home in the United States was in Webster, South Dakota, a pancake-flat stretch of brown prairie land where they didn't know a single person. Mayhoua felt excited, afraid, and confused.

"We were greeted by a huge crowd of Americans from this Lutheran church," Mayhoua said. "We were in the airport. Cameras flashing, TV. Noise. A little boy came and shook my hand and started

The plane that brought Mayhoua's family to the Midwest in 1976 landed in South Dakota. Mayhoua is holding her mother's hand at the top of the stairs.

talking, talking, talking." Mayhoua laughed at the memory. "I thought, here it goes again. I couldn't understand a word."

Mayhoua didn't understand English. "There was no ESL class then. I was in first grade. It helped, going to school . . . but it was a small town. People would stop and greet us. They were so kind. Helpful. But there was not one other Asian person in town. My mother cried every day. They [the townspeople] were kind, but we were so, *so* alone."

Mayhoua's Family Journey

Map by Amelia Janes/Mike Gallagher,
Midwest Educational Graphics

Mayhoua's relatives were scattered from California to Minnesota to South Dakota. Mayhoua's parents wanted to be closer to their relatives. First they moved to California, where they worked picking vegetables. They worked all week and spent weekends outdoors in the mountains together.

Then the family moved to Minnesota, looking for work. "We were trying to get our family back together," Mayhoua said. "My father went to school. To start all over was so difficult."

In Minnesota, Mayhoua had new and painful experiences. "I was older, and realized that when some people—white people—looked at us . . . at any people of color, they didn't see *people,* they saw 'not white.' I remember sitting in the back of the car and some boys spit at our car." Mayhoua felt shaken and afraid.

Children learn new languages easily. Mayhoua was no different. She quickly learned English. But learning to speak a new language is more difficult for adults, like Mayhoua's parents. Mayhoua became her family's **translator** (a person who changes words from one language into another). "By the age of 9, I translated for my parents. I got pulled out of school to translate. . . . I interpreted for my parents at my own parent-teacher conferences!" Mayhoua said. Translating grown-up words and grown-up ideas made Mayhoua feel uncomfortable, but she had no choice.

Mayhoua and her parents were unhappy in Minnesota. In their neighborhood, Hmong boys began to form gangs. Fights broke out. The family decided to move to Wisconsin.

Mayhoua's parents spread out a Wisconsin map. Where should they live? There would be no gangs in small towns. But there would be no other Hmong people there, either. In a big city like Milwaukee, they would have Hmong friends and a Hmong community, but there could be gangs like in Minnesota. They had to choose. They chose Milwaukee.

"Here in Milwaukee with 10,000 Hmong we have fear but we have community," Mayhoua explained. "Community is important. To be Hmong means if I arrived in a strange city with no place to go I would look up a Hmong family in the telephone book and be welcomed into their home."

Hmong people often choose to live in communities near their friends and relatives. Several cities in Wisconsin have large groups of Hmong immigrants.

Today Mayhoua is married to Zongcheng. They have three children: Paylingchia (pie **ling** chee uh), Daechia (**di** chee uh), and Torshia (**tor** see uh). Their beautiful

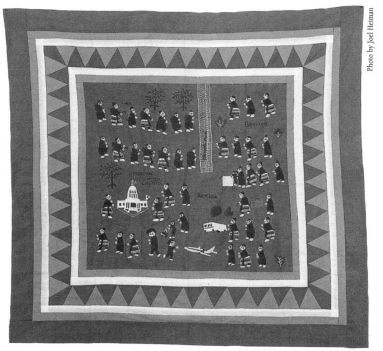

This Hmong story cloth is unusual because it shows the journey from Laos all the way to Madison. Can you find the State Capitol?

names come from Hmong culture. "Paylingchia means new **poppy** [a red flower]," Mayhoua explained. "Daechia means clear water. . . . Torshia, my son . . . his name means mountain highlands."

But Mayhoua fears that even with their Hmong names, her children will forget or ignore their close ties to Hmong culture. "To be Hmong is important," she explained. "But our kids want to be Americans. I fear our culture will be lost . . . all lost.

"You see . . . other people . . . can travel back to Sweden or wherever their homeland is. They can go back. But we have no country. My people . . . moved from place to place. We have [only] our language, our folk stories, our elders . . . our names."

But Mayhoua also has hope. "The name *Hmong* means 'free people.' It also means 'family.' . . . I will say to my children, 'This is your family. You are always Hmong. That is who you are.'"

Looking Back, Looking Forward

The work of making a new life in Wisconsin began long before newcomers arrived on Wisconsin soil. First people had to imagine living a better life. In Unit 1, you learned about some of the main reasons why many

people left their homes. Then people found the courage to pack up and go. In Unit 2, you read about many of the long journeys people took to reach Wisconsin. In this unit, you found that the adventures weren't over once newcomers settled down on a farm or in a town. Getting settled took time. It took hard work on everyone's part, kids as well as parents. Some lucky families began to feel at home in Wisconsin by the end of their first year. Other families took longer. Then there were some, like the Caribbean workers, who never had the opportunity to make Wisconsin their home. Most were luckier. Working hard, learning a new language, and most importantly, finding new friends eased the pain of starting over. You've read many real stories of those who came to Wisconsin. What are the stories your own family tells?

♥ Home, Sweet Wisconsin ♥

Wisconsin is made up of people. Some are Native people whose ancestors lived here. Some are Native people whose families migrated from the eastern United States. Some people came from across the world. Others came across state borders. Families continue to pass down stories of their homelands. They still tell stories of difficult journeys, and they still talk about the first difficult years of settlement in Wisconsin. Being Swiss or Norwegian or Hmong or Mexican or French Canadian is still important to many people. As one German immigrant said, "We're German beneath an American crust."

But when they begin to call Wisconsin *home*, they also become Wisconsinites. Once people begin living here, they cheer for the Packers, eat brats and cheese curds, visit the state capitol in Madison, learn about our history in the classroom, enjoy the first real

In 1984, Jennie Youn Haeng Selder, age four, of Milwaukee, displays her new certificate of naturalization on her father's back. Becoming a U.S. citizen is a big event in people's lives. Being a citizen is one way to tell others that you finally have found the place where you belong.

WHS Archives, CF 6778

snowfall, and look forward to putting away shovels and mittens and heavy jackets in spring.

   People are still coming to Wisconsin. Today, a moving van may pull to the curb in your neighborhood. Who will your new neighbors be? A family from Ohio, Wyoming, India, or Central America? A Mexican American family from south Texas, excited about new jobs and schools? College students from Africa or China, here to study?

   Like millions of others before them, your new neighbors will have to work hard. They will survive homesickness, hard times, and the first long, cold winter. Spring will come. These newcomers will tell their own stories of homelands, journeys, and settling. Their children will remember and pass along the stories. In time, they, too, will call Wisconsin *home*.

Illustration by Jill Bremigan

Wisconsin Locator Map

Ephraim

Oconto

SHAWANO COUNTY

Green Bay

Kewaunee

Shennington

Sparta

Cashton

Manitowoc

Fond du Lac

DODGE COUNTY

On this map are all of the places in Wisconsin where the people in this book lived. Some lived in these places a long time, and some lived there just a little while.

Sauk City

Black Earth

★ Madison

Lake Mills

Milwaukee

Muskego

Prairie du Chien

Racine

Beloit

Clinton

112

Glossary

The pronunciation of each word is shown after the word, like this:

pro • nun • ci • a • tion (prə nun sē a′ shən)

The letters and signs you see in the parentheses should be pronounced as they are in the list below.

The mark ′ is placed after the syllable that requires the most emphasis.

a	hat, cap	**i**	it, pin	**p**	paper, cup	**ə**	sounds like:
ā	age, face	**ī**	ice, five	**r**	run, try		a in about
â	care, fair			**s**	say, yes		e in taken
ä	father, far	**j**	jam, enjoy	**sh**	she, rush		i in pencil
		k	kind, seek	**t**	tell, it		o in lemon
b	bad, rob	**l**	land, coal	**th**	thin, both		u in circus
ch	child, much	**m**	me, am	**ᴛʜ**	then, smooth		
d	did, red	**n**	no, in				
		ng	long, bring	**u**	cup, butter		
e	let, best			** u̇**	full, put		
ē	equal, be	**o**	hot, rock	**ü**	rule, move		
ėr	term, learn	**ō**	open, go				
		ȯ	all, caught	**v**	very, save		
f	fat, if	**ô**	order	**w**	will, woman		
g	go, bag	**oi**	oil, voice	**y**	young, yet		
h	he, how	**ou**	house, out	**z**	zero, breeze		
				zh	measure, seizure		

a • gents (ā′ jənts)   People who arrange deals for others.

am • ne • sty (am′ nə stē)   Official forgiveness.

an • ces • tors (an′ ses tərs)   Relatives who lived long ago.

ar • ti • facts (är′ tə fakts)   Objects like clothing, tools, or toys that people use.

barg • es (bär jz)   Flat boats that carry cargo.

berths (bėrths)   Bunks below deck (or on a train).

blight (blīt)   Disease.

chol • er • a (kol′ ər ə)   A quick-spreading disease that can kill many.

cor • sets (kôr′ sitz)   Stiff underwear designed to give women smaller waists.

deck • hand (dek′ hand)   A worker on a ship.

de • pres • sion (di presh′ ən)   Long-lasting sadness.

des • pe • ra • tion (des pə rā′ shən)   Hopelessness.

des • ti • na • tion (des tə nā′ shən)   Journey's end.

dis • crim • i • na • tion (dis krim ə nā′ shən)   Unfair treatment of people, based on differences such as race, age, or place of birth.

doc • u • ments (dok′ yə mənts)   Printed or handwritten letters, journals, diaries, drawings, or photographs.

drag (drag) A tool pulled across the ground to smooth it.

eld • er (el′ dər) An older and respected member of a tribe or group.

em • i • grants (em′ ə grənts) People who leave one country to move to another.

em • i • grate (em′ ə grāt) To leave one country to move to another.

en • vi • ous (en′ vē əs) Jealous.

es • tate (e stāt′) Landlord's property, or a large area of land, usually with a house on it.

fas • ci • nat • ed (fas′ n ā ted) To be very curious about something.

fic • tion (fik shən) A made-up story.

foul (foul) Rotten.

found • ry (foun′ drē) A factory where metal is melted and shaped.

fresh (fresh) Used to describe a cow that is able to produce milk.

fu • gi • tive (fyü′ jə tiv) Runaway.

green • horns (grēn′ hôrnz) Late-nineteenth- and early-twentieth-century nickname for new arrivals.

grevious *See* grievous.

grieved (grēvd) Felt deeply sad.

griev • ous (grē′ vəs)   Very upset.

grin • gos (gring′ gōs)   Mexican slang for people from the United States.

hatch (hach)   A covered hole in a floor, deck, door, wall, or ceiling.

hire out to work (hīr out tü wėrk)   To work for someone else.

his • to • ri • cal re • sources (hi stôr′ ə kəl ri′ sor siz)   Firsthand information from the time period being studied.

his • tor • y book (his′ tər ē bŭk)   A book that tells about events that really occurred.

il • le • gal (i lē′ gəl)   Not allowed by law.

im • mi • grate (im′ ə grāt)   To arrive in a country to live there permanently.

in • ter • mi • na • ble (in tėr′ mə nə bəl)   Endless.

i • so • lat • ed (ī′ sə lā təd)   Separated from everyone else.

Jim Crow (jim krō)   Separate, for African Americans only.

ko • pek (kō pek)   Small Russian coin.

kro • ner (krō′ nər)   Norwegian money.

lbs.   Abbreviation for pounds.

live • li • hood (līv′ lē hŭd)   Enough money to support oneself.

longjohns (lòng′ jonz)   Long underwear.

Mad • ame (mad′ əm)   In the Sublett story, used to refer to the female slave owner, but more generally a French word for woman.

ma • lar • i • a (mə lâr′ ē ə)   A sickness spread by mosquitoes.

mast (mast)   The tall pole on the deck of a sailing vessel that supports the largest sails.

mem • oirs (mem′ wärz)   Autobiographical stories remembered and written years later.

mi • grants (mī′ grənts)   People who move following work, often traveling north from South Texas, Mexico, and Central America. They move from farm to farm, picking whatever crop is in season.

mi • grate (mī′ grāt)   To move from one community to another in the same country.

min • strel shows (min′ strəl shōz)   American music and dance performances in the 1800s and early 1900s in which musicians and other entertainers would "black" their faces, or put on dark makeup. Such performances made fun of black people.

mis • sion • ar • ies (mish′ ə ner ēz)   People sent by their church or religious groups to teach others about that group's faith.

mourn • ing (môr′ ning)   Feeling deeply sad.

mut • ton (mut′ n)   Meat from a sheep.

Ne • gro (nē′ grō)   Old term for an African American.

pass • ports (pas′ pôrts)   Official travel papers.

pas • tor (pas′ tər)   A minister or priest in charge of a church.

per • ished (per′ ishd)   Died.

per • se • cu • ted (pèr′ sə kyütd)   To be treated cruelly and unfairly because of religion, skin color, or ideas.

pet • ti • coat (pet′ ē kōt)   A slip or underskirt worn under a skirt or dress.

po • groms (pō gromz′)   Organized cruelty and violence against Jews.

pop • py (pop′ ē)   A red flower.

pov • er • ty (pov′ ər tē)   Being very poor.

Prus • sia (prush′ ə)   Once a European country, now a part of Germany and Poland.

put icing on the cake (pùt i′sing on ᴛнə kāk)   Something that changes a situation to make it either much better or much worse.

rab • bi (rab′ ī)   Jewish teacher and leader.

rac • ist (rā′ sist)   A person who treats others cruelly or unfairly because of their race.

re • cruit (ri krüt′)   To try to hire people or to encourage them to join a group or organization.

ref • u • gee (ref yə jē′)   Person forced to leave home because of war or disaster.

ref • u • gee camps (ref yə je′ kamps)   Safe, but not permanent, places for refugees.

Sab • bath (sab′ əth)   Weekly day of rest and worship for some religions, including Judaism. Jews celebrate Sabbath from sundown on Friday night to sundown on Saturday night.

sanc • tu • ar • y (sangk′ chü er ē)   A safe place.

scal • a • wags (scal′ ə wag)   Dishonest people.

schol • ar • ship (skol′ ər ship)   A prize that pays for a student to go to school or college.

schoon • er (skü′ nər)   A type of sailboat widely used on the Great Lakes.

ser • mon (sėr′ mən)   A speech given (usually by the religious leader) during a religious service.

share • crop • pers (shâr′ krop ərz)   Farmers who were so poor that they had no money to rent the land they farmed. To pay the landowner for rent and seed, sharecroppers "shared" or had to pay the landowner part of the money they made from selling their harvested crops.

shil • lings (shil′ ingz)   Coins used in Great Britain until 1971.

skit (skit)   A short play.

smug • gle (smug′ əl)   To bring goods into a country illegally.

spi • der (spī′ dər)   A frying pan with a long handle and legs.

spon • sor (spon′ sər)   Someone who officially offers help or support to a person, group, event, or organization.

squelch • ing (skwel chng)   Sucking or splashing sound.

steer • age (stir′ ij)   In late nineteenth and early twentieth centuries, the portion of the ship where travelers who paid the lowest fares stayed.

stir • ri • bout (stèr′ ə bout)   Oatmeal.

swine (swīn)   Pigs.

syn • a • gogues (sin′ ə gȯgz)   Places where Jews worship.

trea • ty (trē′ tē)   An official agreement between governments.

trans • la • tor (tranz lā′ tər)   A person who changes words from one language into another.

trou • sers (trou′ zərz)   Pants.

tsar (zär)   Also spelled czar. A Russian ruler or emperor before 1918.

un • couth peas • ants (un küth′ pez′ nts)   Poor people without manners or education.

un • ion (yü′ nyən)   An organization of workers set up to help improve things such as working conditions, health benefits, and the amount people are paid to work.

ves • sels (ves′ əls)   Boats or ships.

vom · it · ing (vom′ itng)   Throwing up.

vo · ya · geurs (vwä yä zherz′)   French Canadian boatmen.

wee · vils (wē vəls)   Little bugs that eat grain, cotton, fruit, and other plants and crops.

wretch (rech)   Very sad person.

wretch · ed · ly (rech′ id lē)   Very unhappily.

zwie · back (zwi′ bak)   A kind of dry toast.

Index

This index points to the pages where you can read about persons, places, and ideas. If you do not find the word you are looking for, try to think of another word that means about the same thing.

Sometimes the index will point to another word, like this: Boats. *See* Ships. When you see a **boldface** page number it means there is a picture or map on the page.

Acknowledgments

To my father, who always believes in me. Dad, you're the best! To Robert Elland: thank you for becoming a teacher. You model in your classroom and life the discipline and freedom of art for your students. I want to give special thanks to the Middleton High School artists who contributed to this book and to express my deep appreciation to Maria Covarrubias, Mayhoua Moua, and the gracious women of the Historical Committee of the Mohican Nation, Stockbridge-Munsee Band, for the gift of their stories and words to me and to Wisconsin's children.

I would like to thank the following Society staff members for their work on this book: Bobbie Malone, acquisitions editor; Margaret T. Dwyer, developmental editor; Kathryn Thompson, managing editor; Jill Bremigan, book designer; Deborah T. Johnson, production manager; James Feldman, Joel Heiman, and Catherine Johnson, research assistants. The cartographic talents of Amelia Janes and Michael Gallagher and the illustrations of Susan Manske and Jill Bremigan also added great vitality to the text. The sage advice and expert guidance of Landon Risteen, volunteer to the Office of School Services and longtime Society member, added greatly to the structure of *They Came to Wisconsin*.

A generous gift from Hugh Highsmith Family Foundation helped support this publication.

They Came to Wisconsin **Reviewer List**

Emery Babcock
Stevens Point Public Schools

Staci Basting
Eau Claire Area School District

Brad Bliss
Knapp Elementary School
Racine

Halema Caldwell
Brown St. Elementary
Milwaukee

Jules Cappelle
Monticello School District

Carol Cardinal
Lac du Flambeau Elementary
Lac du Flambeau

Geri Cupery
Madison Public Library

Dorothy Davids
Mohican Nation
Stockbridge-Munsee Band

Heidi Ebert
West Salem Elementary School

Patricia Fettes
Flambeau School District

Kira Fobbs
Lincoln Elementary
Madison

Anne Gassere
Franklin Elementary School
Oshkosh

Karen Gierzak
Fort Atkinson School District

Steven Grusznski
Elcho Elementary School

Agnes Keller
School District of Crandon

J. P. Leary
Department of Public Instruction
Madison

Mike Madden
Sevastopol School
Sturgeon Bay

Rick Martinson
West Salem Elementary School

Donna Nosek
Lincoln Elementary School
Whitewater Unified School District

Marilyn Penn
Royal Oaks Elementary School
Sun Prairie

Joy-Lyn Rehm
95th Street Elementary School
Milwaukee

Linda Reuvers
East Elementary School
New Richmond

Landon Risteen
Consultant
Chicago, Illinois

Karin Seefeldt
Greenwood Elementary School
River Falls School District

Linda Toonen
University of Wisconsin–
Green Bay

Mark Waggoner
Elmore Elementary School
Green Bay